I0491414

STUDENTS' SLICK WAY OF SAVING MONEY

LEARN TO SAVE MONEY, CURB OVERSPENDING HABITS, AND BECOME A DEBT-FREE GRADUATE!

JAN KAISER

To all my readers: Thinking of our crazy, fun, awkward, boring, silly, yet wonderful years as a student. I guarantee you won't go "hangry" again!

(The checklist you can't afford to go without...)

This checklist includes:

- Top 11+ side hustle ideas for a student.
- Most recommended budgeting apps to start mapping your finances.
- Sites worth visiting for free or inexpensive textbooks, school supplies, & housing essentials.

Don't go another school year unaware of your financial situation, overspending on things you could have gotten for free, or at a ridiculous low price!

For easy access, please visit the QR code in your gift box below.

CONTENTS

INTRODUCTION

High school and college is a special time in everyone's life. To begin with, graduating by itself is a measure of how successful you'll be in life. To enter college you need to have worked hard at the high school level, whether related to your grades or in sports. As a student, you spend a lot of your time ensuring you achieve good grades in your subjects, and this is time well spent!

Your priorities at this point probably involve getting good grades and having an active social life. Sure, you want to land a great job and start a successful career once you leave school, but these are great reasons why grades matter. High school and college teach you many lessons every step of the way however, there's one thing that you may be sorely ignorant of: Money.

When you go to college, your tuition is probably being taken care of by either your parents or some form of financial aid or a combination of both. You're probably working a job on campus, but that just gives you money to spend on the weekends. College is often referred to as being the final playpen in a person's life, and the way the average college student thinks about money bears this out.

You could also be in high school worried about what your financial future is going to look like. The prospect of student loan debt might be towering over you, and you might not feel that there are too many options for you to make money, and start becoming more independent. You're technically treated like a kid in high school, but sooner than later you will have to face the responsibilities that come with being an adult.

The statement 'broke student' probably resonates with you. These days, many students assume student loan debt in order to fund their education. If this happens to be you, I have some news for you: You're not broke. You're on a path that will put you in a place where you're far worse than broke.

Debt among students in America has reached alarming levels. The current amount of student loan debt is $1.6 trillion (Friedman, 2020). The average student carries a debt of $32,371, which translates to a payment of $393 per month after graduation.

This doesn't sound like much, but remember that this is the average number. If you happen to go to a private university, your payments will be a lot higher. Upon graduation, the average student earns a salary of $48,500 (Hess, 2020). This translates to an average income of $3,200 per month.

This means your student loan debt payment is more than 10% of your take home pay. Odds are that your first car loan payment is going to be cheaper than what you pay on student loan debt! If you live in a big city such as New York or San Francisco, $3,200 won't even get you your own place to live in.

While there are systemic issues that are causing student loan debt levels to increase massively, a bigger issue is the fact that the average college student knows nothing about personal finance. For the most part, such courses aren't a part of the required curriculum.

As a result, students focus entirely on their grades and think that the salaries they'll earn once they graduate will take care of all their debt burden. They arrive in the real world to find that this is grossly untrue and that they've just wasted four years' time spending money when they could have paid down a lot of their debt while still in school.

BUDGETING

Common money advice that is given to students runs something along the lines of 'you need a budget - so budget!' If you're anything like how I was in my college aged years, then this statement means nothing to you. Sure, you can create a budget with a few line items on it, but how do you actually use the budget to improve your finances?

A budget teaches you to reduce your expenses at best. However, you can't go through life simply reducing your expenses at every turn. You need to figure out how to make money as well. Learning how to save is the first step and in this book, and I'm going to teach you what real saving looks like.

It doesn't matter whether your financial situation is desperate or if you're simply looking to save up for a single, special purchase. I'm here to tell you that everyone can save money, no matter how little you think you have in the bank. My objective isn't to tell you to have less fun or to cut down your spending on unnecessary items. You know that already! Instead, I'm going to focus on showing you how you can not only save but make more money by creating some simple mental shifts. These will help you emerge from college debt-free and will set you up for the rest of your life.

Here's a little test you can take right now to gauge the level of your financial literacy. You've just learned that the average student will earn around $3,200 per month upon graduation and that their debt will be more than 10% of this figure. What's your reaction to this?

Are you thinking that 10% isn't so bad? After all, the salary is four figures and the debt payment is just three figures. It can't be that bad! This is a pretty good indication that you need a book like this to educate you. You need to learn that, in the real world, expenses add up quickly and that 10% is a pretty significant chunk!

What's more, thanks to the way interest works, you're going to end up paying a lot more than the sticker price of your education. Interest here refers to the financial term, not the regular English word. Interest is something I have a lot of experience with as you'll see!

My Story

Like many Americans, I come from an immigrant family. My parents moved to America a few months before September 11, 2001. We had a pretty traditional familial structure. My father was the provider while my mother took care of things at home. As kids, my brother and I were expected to study hard and get good grades.

Being the elder child, my experience growing up was sometimes difficult. I was the only person at home who could explain, to my parents and my brother, how the education system worked in the United States. I had to figure out a lot of things for myself but I'm grateful for this experience because it has made me a lot tougher.

I figured out that while grades are important, the real challenge comes after high school. I graduated with a weighted GPA of 4.4 and my objective was to attend college. I even enrolled in a dual enrollment program in high school (you'll learn more about it in Chapter 7). Sure, a lot of people told me that Mark Zuckerberg never finished college. Well, he didn't need to! But college, for most people, is like depositing money in their pocket.

It might be a piece of paper to some but no one can ever take that achievement away from you. These days, many students believe that college is a waste of time due to the number of money making opportunities available online. This is not true at all. Sure, you might be overpaying for college but to brand the entire collegiate experience as being worthless is a bit extreme.

My first taste of financial interest began with the college orientations my high school hosted. I couldn't make heads or tails of the numbers being thrown at me, and I was far more interested in figuring out which school looked the coolest and had the best activities I could get involved in.

My father was the one who figured out all the numbers and during college visits; I simply spent my time gawking at the campus buildings and wondering where the cool parties were. Chances are, you did, or would do the same! I ended up choosing a college in West Palm Beach due to the fact that the instructors seemed really knowledgeable and were actual professionals in the industry.

Everything was great! Right until the day I learned that the university had been sold to another one. I didn't know universities did that! Upon arriving, I was told that I would not be allowed access to my dorm unless I paid the fees upfront. This was $10,000 for four months! I didn't understand at the time how expensive this was.

I was told that I didn't qualify for student aid (even though I thought I did) and that I would have to assume a loan to finance this amount. I didn't want to burden my parents excessively and in an attempt to prove how responsible I was, I ended up signing a loan which carried an interest rate of 10%!

In a way, this ridiculous interest rate was a blessing because it helped me work out the numbers and see that I was being robbed. Soon, this payment became impossible to manage. I left the university shortly and enrolled in a community college and earned my associate's degree in Business Administration. After earning my AA, I transferred to Florida International University (whose school of business was ranked fifth in the nation at the time) and worked towards a dual degree in logistics and supply chain management.

Throughout all of this, I learned the value of living for free. My parents had given me that life and I realized how lucky I was to not have to worry about money when I was growing up. Today, I'm debt-free and have a great career working in logistics. This book is a collection of all the lessons I learned as a student.

I aim to help you become confident of assessing your financial situation once you're done reading this book. Outside influences are playing a huge role in how you spend money right now and I'm going to show you how you can take control of it.

Debt is a horrible thing to accumulate and the time to act is right now! You might not fully understand the repercussions of accumulating interest on your debt fully, but you can understand when I say that you'll be paying almost three times the stated price of your tuition for a long time after you've graduated!

This is your chance to be one of the few students that graduate without any debt. You will also learn what to do in order to save for that dream car, home or vacation!

You've taken a great step in purchasing this book. It shows that you're serious about taking charge of your money. Now take that step further and educate yourself as to how exactly you can do it!

1

WHY SAVE MONEY?

W hat's the big deal with saving money in the first place? If you earn $100 and if your expenses are under that, there's no issue right? You can pay for your living expenses and you can always find a source of money these days.

These words approximate what the average high school or college student thinks about money and how it needs to be used. It isn't their fault they think this way. They've never been told otherwise or shown how incorrect this thought process is. When growing up, we're never exposed to what it takes to earn money.

We're either given it by our parents or we work part-time jobs to earn a few bucks here and there. While this teaches us how to work, it doesn't teach us anything about the responsibility of balancing expenses with income or how important saving is.

How often do you view your paycheck (if you work at a part-time job currently) as a license to spend money? Do you see it as being free money? You might save a few dollars here and there but how often do you take the time to ask yourself whether you ought to be saving more and spending less?

I know I certainly didn't when I was in high school and college! Before getting into the 'how' of saving money, it's important for you to understand the 'why.' After all, you need to know why you're doing something before doing it! You might have picked up this book to learn how to reduce your level of debt but saving money has bigger reasons than this.

WHY YOU NEED TO SAVE MONEY

There are many advantages to saving money and while the physical benefits of it are the most apparent ones, the real benefits occur mentally. What I mean is that, when you have money, your brain literally changes into a more peaceful state. Let's look at the various things that occur when you begin saving money.

Peace of Mind

How would you like to wake up in the morning without worrying about how you're going to pay for next month's rent or for food? At this moment, if you run out of money you might be able to pick up the phone and ask your parents for some. However, there's going to come a time when you won't be able to do this anymore.

You might be focusing exclusively on getting good grades before you graduate high school or college at the moment, but grades alone aren't going to help you pay your bills right now! All the worries highlighted in the previous paragraph might soon haunt you!

Do you have enough money in the bank right now to pay for your expenses? Imagine a situation where you couldn't call anyone and needed to figure out how you're going to pay for your living expenses. This brings up quite a lot of anxiety, doesn't it? Now imagine having enough in the bank to pay for a year's worth of expenses.

Saving money frees your mind and this in turn frees you up to live however you want. If you don't save enough money, you'll eventually find yourself spending solely on your needs and not indulging enough of your wants. (You'll learn more about needs and wants shortly.)

For now, remember that your peace of mind is paramount. It's what allows you to express the best version of yourself and to build a better life.

More Options

Having money in the bank literally gives you options. It allows you to take more risks since you have a healthy cushion to fall back on. Imagine a situation where you're working at a job you're not exactly pleased with and want to start your own business. If you happen to have enough money saved up to pay for your living expenses for a year, you can exercise your option to quit and start a business.

The peace of mind you'll have when starting a new business will help you navigate the stress better. You'll be able to focus entirely on your new business without worrying about paying for your usual expenses.

It isn't just about starting a new business. Money in the bank allows you to go on that exotic vacation. If you have enough saved up, you can even buy yourself something that is ridiculously expensive. All of us have irrational wants that we cannot justify. We're often told that we should ignore these urges as much as possible.

Well, indulging these urges is what makes life worth living. I'm not saying you should indulge all of them. However, treating yourself to one of these wants now and then is a great way to be happy and feel satisfied. Money that you can afford to spend (truly afford) gives you this freedom.

Building Wealth

Money does this wonderful thing where if you put it to work sensibly, it goes away and comes back with even more friends. This additional money can also be put to work and in turn, this creates more money. Welcome to the world of compounding interest.

. . .

Here's an example of how it works. Let's say you put together $1,000 and invest it in an opportunity that returns $100 every year. That's a 10% return which happens to be a very high rate of return for an investment. $100 doesn't sound like much, does it? It's barely $8 per month! That's one meal at a fast food joint.

However, let's assume that you never need to touch your principal (which is $1,000) ever again. You simply leave it in this investment and let it grow. After five years, this investment will be worth $1,610. After 10 years, it's $2593.74. That's a gain of 160%. Averaged over 10 years, you've made around 16% per year.

However, your investment pays just 10%. In effect, you've been earning a free six percent per year! How great is that? The amounts might not be impressing you very much. Consider the scenario where your principal balance was $40,000 instead of $1,000. In this case, you'll end up with an amount of $103,750 at the end of 10 years.

$40,000 might sound like a lot of money and you might stare at your bank balance of just a few dollars and think you'll never have that much. Well, don't sweat it at this point. I'll be showing you how you can make money as well as be saving more of it. At this point, it's important for you to understand the power of compounding and how it gives you free money.

This should also help you understand how you're losing a lot more on frivolous spending than just the amount you pay. Let's say you buy a pair of shoes that you don't really need and pay $100 for them. You might reason that $100 isn't much and you can always work more hours and make it back.

Well, $100 invested at 10% for 10 years turns into $260. So, really, you're losing at least two and a half times the amount you spent on those shoes. Imagine withdrawing $260 in cash from your bank and flushing it down the toilet. That's what you're doing.

Now imagine borrowing money to pay for those shoes. Let's say after interest, you end up paying $150 for them or 50% more than what they're selling for. $150 invested at 10% for 10 years turns into $390. Now, you're losing close to four times what those shoes are selling for!

This is what debt does. It magnifies your losses. I must mention that there are some forms of debt that are helpful. Debt by itself isn't bad. It's the decision to use debt in certain circumstances that is good or bad. At some point, using debt to finance your education is bad.

This happens when you can't afford to make payments or if your expected salary won't cover living expenses thanks to your debt burden. Think in terms of building wealth instead of thinking about merely income versus expenses. The money you save is extremely powerful and will work for you.

. . .

The best part is that compound interest is fully automatic. You don't need to do anything additional to make it happen. It's just a law of nature. Use the compound interest calculator at

http://www.moneychimp.com/calculator/ compound_interest_calculator.htm and play around with it to see how powerful it can be.

Travel Opportunities

Would you like to study abroad? Would you like to take that spring break vacation to Acapulco or even the south of France? Travel is something that many people save up for and is one of the most fulfilling experiences you can have in life. It literally opens up new worlds for you.

Having money in the bank opens this world of opportunities for you. It gives you something to look forward to as well. By ignoring your finances and rejecting the notion of saving, you're shrinking the world that is available for you to explore.

WANTS AND NEEDS

It is important to have a specific mind-set to attain a rewarding lifestyle. Avoid being oblivious of your surroundings just because you get caught up in the moment. be aware of your actions and of those around you at all times. In other words, be present when you are making decisions, especially when you are making financial decisions. Please note that when we talk about financial decisions we are talking about choices that involve money.

Many forget to be present at all times, I get it. Oftentimes fun overrides our common senses, but we need to take control and learn to have smart fun instead. That will stop you from the committing errors that can truly harm your pockets. The most basic error ... on things that you do not need.

A good example of this is a person who feels as if they absolutely have to have the new iPhone 1000 or whatever number the latest edition is. They see all these people on Instagram flashing it about and marvel at the cool ads that play on TV. Unfortunately, they have just $100 in the bank.

Instead of stepping away from the purchase, they instead try to figure out how they can afford something that sells for $600 by paying just $100. Debt is the answer! What's more, they're told that they can 'always refinance.' How wonderful is that! It is truly wonderful how the concept of refinancing sinks more people into even more debt than anything else.

There are a lot of mental phenomena going on in this situation but the first thing to understand is the notion of needs versus wants. Basically, a need is something you have to have in order to survive. Food is a need, as is rent money. Water is a need as is exercise. Clothes and utility bills are needs and if you're living in an area where public transportation or walking is not an option, a vehicle is a need as is the gas money for it.

A want is an item that energizes you but isn't really needed from a survival perspective. You want to go to the south of France. Sure, you'll be disappointed if you don't go but is it really going to put your life in jeopardy if you don't go? You want that Ferrari or equivalent Tesla 32, but is not getting it going to threaten your very existence? Unlikely.

People often end up spending too much on wants because they're exaggerated versions of needs. For example, you need a place to live. However, you want a big house. You need to spend time with friends and socialize. Do you have to spend hundreds of dollars on entertainment and fancy clothes every weekend? Many people in college do exactly this in the name of having a social life and end up costing themselves money.

Wants, of course, inject some fun into your life. It is fun to buy that new dress or that new phone. However, understand that the 'fun' that you experience is a biological process. You can hack this process and feel the same levels of joy without spending as much money.

Let's look at how this works.

Having Fun With Less

Why do you feel the need to stare at social media all day long? Why are those Instagram or TikTok posts of your favorite influencer so captivating? This is because your brain releases a neurotransmitter called dopamine (Julson, 2018). Dopamine is a chemical that has several important functions in our bodies.

It is effectively a signal for our brain to experience pleasure, increase memory, attention and it even governs the way our body moves. The more dopamine an activity releases, the more you're programming yourself to do whatever it is that is increasing dopamine levels.

This is why changing your habits is hard and pure willpower doesn't cut it. What you need to do instead is figure out how to generate dopamine in ways that don't involve indulging in harmful habits. Let's look at an example of this.

Let's say you're sick of eating ramen all day and are really craving for something delicious. You go online and find that there's a great deal for Korean barbecue for just $25. It's all you can eat as well so the $25 price tag seems justified. At this point you have a choice to make.

You can either go ahead and spend the $25 (which is actually $65 when compounded, as we discussed previously) or you can remind yourself of why you're cooking at home in the first place. Your 'whys' are extremely important and they're what help you remain disciplined in the long-term.

A simple meal outside will satisfy you to a much larger extent than it normally would if you ate it regularly. Figure out your 'whys' and you'll find that you'll derive a lot of pleasure from indulging in your wants to a far lesser degree. This is how you remain disciplined and temper excessive spending on wants.

.   .   .

You can even justify spending on certain wants by cutting down on your spending on others. Let's say you cannot get by without nice-looking clothes and that your clothing budget is higher than what someone who merely 'needs' clothes would spend. Well, you can buy yourself better clothes but cut down on spending on meals outside.

It all ties back to what your 'whys' are. Choosing the 'whys' that are the most important is what will keep you on track and will enforce discipline in you. Take some time right now to figure out the following:

1. Why are you reading this book?
2. Why are these reasons important to you? Make them as detailed as possible.
3. What are your needs?
4. What are your wants? List them and rank them in order of importance.
5. Starting from the highest want, list out why this want is important and why it's more pleasurable than the one below it.

This isn't an exercise you can complete in a few minutes. Technically you can scribble whatever you want but if you want real results, you'll need to take the time to really figure out what moves you.

AWARENESS

How do you keep track of your spending and of those times when you're close to the edge of breaking your discipline? Discipline often invokes images of some kind of restriction but nothing could be further from the truth. Discipline is what frees you in the long run. Regarding your finances, having disciplined spending habits is what allows you to save more money. This allows you to indulge in things you really want and gives you greater freedom.

A key component of remaining disciplined is to remove any opportunity you might have to break your discipline. For example, if you've decided to cook at home and eat out just once a week, having a ready snack for when you get hungry is being prepared. This way, you won't find yourself in a position where you'll be hungry, which means you might break your discipline.

In short, you need to prepare. Preparation is a result of awareness. Awareness in turn requires you to take a deep look at yourself, both positively and negatively. I'm not saying you need to berate yourself here! Instead, you need to honestly assess your weak points and figure out the scenarios in which you're likely to become less disciplined.

Are cupcakes your weak point? If you were to walk past a row of cupcakes, would you be incapable of resisting a purchase? Awareness of this beforehand will help you avoid this situation in the first place. It's far easier to avoid bad situations than it is to overcome them. Simply remove yourself from the game instead of trying to figure out how you can avoid losing!

Take the time now to create a list of situations that cause you to spend more money than is wise. Your goal here is to analyze your habits that lead to the situation being created. For example, do you visit shopping centers or fancy stores when you get bored? Instead of visiting these places, find something else to keep yourself occupied. Even if you do go, leave your wallet at home, or just bring a limited amount of cash.

Awareness of your habits is extremely powerful and taking the time to examine them will help you avoid many bad situations.

Gratitude

Gratitude is something that has an unbelievably positive effect on your life and mindset. It's a bit like a superhero serum since it improves the quality of your relationships, your emotional health and physical health in one go. Research shows that gratitude also helps boost your immune system and you're less likely to fall sick as a result (Luenendonk, 2016).

What does gratitude have to do with spending and saving money? Quite a lot actually! Many of us spend a lot of time on social media and it is close to impossible to remain in touch with people these days if you avoid it. While there are a few individuals who carry flip phones and have eliminated social media from their lives, most of us would not find this practical.

Instead of trying to avoid it, add discipline to your consumption. It's pretty easy to limit your social media activity to just an hour or two every day. If you're using it to make money, then use it to make money and not to catch up on gossip or e-stalk someone. This latter behavior is something all of us engage in, to some degree, and it usually only causes us to feel worse about ourselves.

This is where gratitude comes into the picture. Someone who is pleased with where their lives are at right now will not have any reason to envy someone else's perfect seeming life on Instagram or Facebook. It will allow them to view things from the proper perspective.

Gratitude will also help you shift your perspective on your financial situation. I'm not talking about reminding yourself of how someone has it worse. Sure, there are kids starving in some parts of the world who have it worse than you but this hardly makes you feel better about yourself!

What gratitude really does is it helps you focus on the things you do have, instead of adopting an attitude of lack and desperate need. For example, instead of thinking about how you cannot afford a lot of nice things, you could look at what you already have and feel grateful for having them. Once you begin to evaluate what you have, you'll realize that their many things you do have that are pretty amazing! You'll realize that, more often than not, there's no need for you to spend money on buying new things. You already have a lot of things that you need!

Here are some other ways in which gratitude helps:

1. Social connection - Human beings need to form relationships with those around them. Gratitude helps us connect with those around us and build better and more fulfilling relationships. It will help you achieve a sense of belonging which is far more important that the temporary validation that an expensive purchase brings.

2. Improved self-esteem - Gratitude gets you to focus on the positives in your life. Do this long enough and you'll begin to see all the great things you've created in your own life through your efforts. This will boost your confidence in yourself and you'll need less validation from external sources.

3. Reduces stress - Stress has a direct impact on your expenses. You're more likely to make poor decisions under stress and your health will deteriorate as well. Aside from increased medical expenses, no one wants to live under a constant cloud of sickness!

4. Encourages learning - One of the key qualities that boosts learning efforts is curiosity. You cannot be curious if you're constantly focused on how things are terrible for you. This attitude is at odds with the state

of enthusiasm that learning demands. Developing gratitude will ensure you score better grades!

5. Enhanced problem solving - The stuff you learn will in-turn help you solve problems in your life in better ways. What's more, embracing gratitude will help you avoid making bad decisions that create those problems. This means you'll have more energy to figure out better ways to save money and address the problems in your life.

6. Increased motivation - If you're feeling good about yourself, you're going to be more motivated to achieve results in your life. You'll be willing to work harder and reach the goals you set for yourself. This is extremely relevant when it comes to figuring out ways to make more money. You'll need to be creative and work hard to achieve results and gratitude will help you get there.

How to Develop Gratitude

Perhaps the best part about gratitude is that it doesn't take anything special to harness it. The reason you might feel it's tough is because you're allowing your negative impression to cloud your judgment. At the end of every day, take the time to list five things you're deeply grateful for.

You're, I hope, extremely lucky to be living in an environment where you have the support of a community, your parents as well as your teachers. What would your world look like if you had to worry about where your next meal was going to come from? If you had to worry about finding a place to sleep at night instead of worrying about homework? Look around you and you'll find many things to be grateful for. Even just little things, like having a nice slice of pizza, or enjoying the company of your friends.

Take around 15 minutes to compile this list. In addition to this, write down a compliment to yourself. What did you do well during the day and which action of yours impressed you the most? It could literally be anything. You're not judging yourself by doing this, but rather noticing good things about yourself.

The idea is to simply examine the positives in your life. The more you look at them, the more you'll focus on them. The more you focus on them, the better your life will be and the better your decisions will be. The better your decisions are, the less bad ones you'll make and your problems will automatically reduce or solve themselves.

ANYONE CAN DO IT

Right now, saving money might seem like a kind of "old-fashioned" task to you. Don't worry, this is a normal feeling to have. I'm here to tell you that improving your financial situation and saving money is not rocket science. It's simply a matter of looking at the positives in your life and appreciating them.

Understand that unless you figure out your 'whys' and develop gratitude for what you already have, no method is going to work well for you. You might get lucky and have something work out but this is a bit like relying on the lottery to get rich. It's not sustainable and is a bad way to go about building your finances.

So, before focusing on the methods, focus on yourself. After all, you're the common thread through your entire life. It stands to reason that before you change your external results, you need to set up things correctly internally.

Let me also make it clear that it isn't only those who make lots of money who are in a position to save it. It's true that making more money makes saving it easy. However, regardless of your circumstances, you can save money. It doesn't matter if you save just a few dollars at first. Don't get down on yourself for saving just a small amount.

Instead, look at it as a victory. The smallest of amounts can snowball into a huge sum of money when you do things correctly!

2

HOW TO SPEND LESS AND ENJOY MORE OF YOUR MONEY

Enjoying your money is a matter of perspective. One of my friends graduated from college and began working full-time and gained a bit of a reputation. To be frank, it wasn't the most flattering one! She was often teased by her colleagues (good naturedly) about how she wore the same five outfits to work and how she rarely spent much money on company happy hours.

Her entertainment options were also frugal and involved walking around parks and going to museums and other free attractions instead of visiting fancy restaurants or buying new clothes. Oh yeah, her car was a bit of a beater as well!

So, what did all of this frugality get her? Well, she saved half of her salary every year and soon had saved up enough to go on a sabbatical for a year and live in Paris! Which experience do you think she found more enjoyable? Living in Paris for a year without a care in the world or buying some temporary piece of fashion that social media was telling her was cool?

The answer is obvious. The tool she used to plan all of this was a budget. A budget is an extremely powerful thing and it also happens to be the one that most people get wrong. Most students don't even bother creating a budget. You might not feel the pinch right now, especially if your folks are subsidizing you, but I can guarantee that you will set yourself up for financial ruin if you carry this behavior into the real world.

College and high school give you the perfect sandbox in which you can create a budget and take various methods out for a spin. Even if you fail, the consequences are not extremely negative and you can afford to make a few mistakes. Why is budgeting so powerful? I mean, it's just a list of expenses right? How much power can a list have?

Instead of looking at your budget as a list, look at it as a framework for your finances. It defines your cash flowing in and your cash flowing out. You can increase the first and decrease the second factor and this is how financial freedom is attained. You can do things like live in Paris for a year or two once you have financial freedom. How does that sound for a goal?

Before getting into the details of how to create a budget, let's take a quick look at some common mistakes that people make before they even create one.

MISTAKES TO AVOID

The biggest mistake you want to avoid is to not have a budget. The thing that prevents people from creating a budget is to think that they don't need one or even worse, believe they can keep track of their spending in their heads. I can assure you that no matter how great your memory is, there is no way you'll be able to keep track of every single cent you spend.

You might get away with it for now but in the future, this bad habit will come back to bite you. Another mistake that occurs when creating a budget is to guess the amounts you spend on certain things and then neglect to track it. For example, you might allocate $250 per month to groceries and then forget about it. However, you could be spending as much as $500 in this category.

Tracking is an essential part of budgeting and you need to develop a system that allows you to track your expenses as you incur them. You can do this by using an app that connects to your bank accounts or you can do them manually by saving your receipts and then entering them into a spreadsheet.

Given that budgeting involves discipline, it's quite common to see people neglect to account for entertainment expenses. Spending time socializing or catching a movie are things that most of us enjoy. However, if you don't allocate money to such expenses, you'll find yourself reaching a boiling point and then splurging on these expenses.

It's a bit like going grocery shopping when you're hungry. You're bound to buy stuff you don't need because your hunger warps your decision-making abilities. Remember, it's far better to avoid placing yourself in bad situations than it is to overcome bad ones as they occur.

Your monthly bills are recurring costs so it might seem as if they're fixed. For example, it's easy to forget that your monthly cell phone bill is not a fixed cost but is one that you have assumed to be so. It's an easy mistake to make so make sure you clearly indicate the areas in your budget where you can save money.

Don't carry this out to an extreme, though. I mean, you could save a ton of money by not eating food. However, this is hardly a practical solution, is it? The aim is to reduce your expenses and not to torture yourself! Entertainment is something that always gets cut when people try to save money.

Instead of cutting it out completely, look to scale it back. Instead of going out every night, why not opt for different activities that don't cost anything? Can you spend less money when you meet your friends after school? I'll cover more of this in the tips section at the end of this chapter. For now, just keep in mind that eliminating entertainment expenses is a bad choice.

Lastly, remember to build an emergency fund. This fund will pay for unforeseen expenses, such as the cost of a new phone or a laptop. Fix a certain amount in your mind and contribute a certain amount towards this every month. Remember that this contribution is over and above your regular savings!

PREPARING A BUDGET

There are two broad ways you can utilize to prepare a budget. The first is to adopt the manual approach and input everything into a spreadsheet. The second is to use an app. Both methods have their advantages and disadvantages. There's no need to overthink this. Try each one and see which one suits you best.

Some people prefer the manual method because it puts you in direct touch with your money. You'll be entering receipts yourself and you'll be able to see exactly how much you're spending immediately. Apps tend to be a bit remote no matter how many notifications they send you.

However, they're fully customizable and make goal planning easy. For example, if your goal is to save for an emergency fund, you can program this into the app and it will automatically let you know how much money you have in that particular basket. This is a very useful thing to have.

Line Items

What are your monthly expenses? List all of them out. If you're still in high school, you might not have too many expenses of your own. Keep the list below in mind since this is what you'll likely have to pay for in the near future.

For most people, the list will cover all expenses:

- Rent
- Utilities
- Debt payment
- Car payment/ transportation
- Exercise/gym membership
- Phone
- Cable/internet
- Groceries
- Insurance (car and health)
- Emergency fund contribution
- Entertainment
- Any other contribution
- Personal grooming
- Miscellaneous

A lot of these items are flexible in terms of cost. The thing you need to do is to begin with the fixed costs and list their amounts out first. Rent, car payments, insurance, memberships etc. tend to be fixed so these are pretty straightforward to fix.

When it comes to variable costs, it helps to break them down by the amounts you'll spend every time you indulge in them. For example, your entertainment might consist of going to the movies and meeting up with friends. You can set a fixed amount of money that you want to spend every time you do this and then multiply that by the number of times you do it.

Keep in mind that you can reduce these costs if you need to. For example, you might decide to watch a movie twice a month instead of every week. Opting for a service like Netflix might also reduce your cable bill as well as your movie watching bills. So, evaluate all your options here.

Once again, keep in mind that the idea here is to arrive at a total number that allows you to live comfortably within your means. Your objective should not be to punish yourself by cutting out everything that isn't a need. Things that aren't needs should be minimized and not eliminated.

If you don't do this, you'll only be setting yourself up to violate your budget when an opportunity arises.

Tracking

Now comes the tough part. Once you've set up your line items, you need to track your spending in each category. The best way to track expenses is to record them the minute you incur them. If you're tracking your expenses manually, you need to save your receipts and then enter them every day, or as soon as you can.

Budget Goals

While setting up a budget and tracking how you spend money is great, what should be your objectives when it comes to saving money? Here are the three most important goals you should be hitting first before you even think of spending large amounts of money on wants, or taking on additional debt:

1. Reduce any existing debt, as quickly as possible
2. Save at least six months' worth of living expenses
3. Build an emergency fund through regular contribution

Reducing debt should be your first priority. As you've already learned in the previous chapter, debt has the capacity to double your losses when you take lost compounded income into account. Consolidate your debt as much as possible and don't draw other lines of credit if you're already carrying debt.

For example, if you're carrying student loan debt, don't apply for a credit card, no matter how amazing the rewards are. Credit card rewards do save you a lot of money when used right. However, you're still carrying debt. This means the good cards will be out of your reach. Secondly, you're a student. The probability of finding good cards that offer great deals are low, trust me.

The next point to keep in mind is to save six months' worth of living expenses as cash. What you then want to do is invest these funds into a CD or in a savings account. If you think your circumstances are shaky, you're better off sticking to a savings account since these don't have as many withdrawal penalties.

A CD or a certificate of deposit pays you interest on the sums you invest. However, you need to keep your money invested in it for a certain period of time. Withdrawing or 'breaking' the CD before the term ends results in penalties being applied. Terms can range from six months to six years.

Invest in them only if you're absolutely certain you won't need the money for the term you choose. This is why I mentioned that if you believe your situation is shaky, you should invest your emergency cash in a savings account since there are no penalties associated with them.

Doing this will give a good cushion where you don't need to worry about losing your job. It also gives you the freedom to quit a job if you think it isn't a great fit for you or if you wish to prioritize your studies more. It's best to line up another job in advance before deciding to move on from the current one if you plan on continuing to work.

Lastly, you want to rotate this amount. What I mean is that once you have six months' worth of expenses saved up, you need to withdraw one month's worth of expenses and live on that amount strictly. As your income comes in, replenish the six-month fund accordingly. This way, you'll set up a system where your living expenses for a month are preset and this will make it easier to follow your goals.

Good and Bad Debt

I've mentioned earlier how debt by itself isn't a bad thing. Instead, it is the decision that drives the assumption of debt that is good or bad. There are many forms of good debt you can undertake. For example, drawing a mortgage (which is a loan from a bank to buy a house) in order to collect rental payments is an example of a good debt. Also, owning a home, and having a reasonable mortgage on it, is a way to build money by the increases in the values of homes over time.

A good rule of thumb to apply is to ask yourself if your wealth will increase if you assume the debt. Student loan debt is good to assume if the skills you learn will bring you a job that pays you a high salary that can eliminate the debt. However, if at all possible, it's best to avoid student debt of any kind. It's almost impossible, for example, to have it "forgiven" if you run into hard times - for instance, even if you have to declare bankruptcy, the student loan debt never goes away.

If the salary is too low then it isn't worth it as an investment, no matter how passionate you are about studying the subject. You're better off working a job elsewhere and saving up money to study the subject instead.

Credit card debt is another example of bad debt. Payday loans and salary advance loans are even worse. The interest rates on these loans are ridiculously high and you're only borrowing from the future to pay the present. Eventually, all that accumulated debt will add up and you'll be left with nothing.

A good rule of thumb is to not carry more than one line of debt in your portfolio. That's right, you need to think of yourself as a money manager who is managing assets. These assets and money are yours, and you must pay attention to them. If you have student loan debt, don't carry credit cards; except in extreme circumstances. For example, when interacting with unavoidable places where only credit cards are accepted. In this case you might want to carry only one card with a credit limit of $1,000 and do not spend more than 30% of that amount. However, I would encourage you to avoid these circumstances all together.

COMMON CREDIT CARD MISTAKES

Aside from assuming them when you have other lines of debt, credit cards open up the possibility of committing a number of mistakes that will reduce your wealth, for sure. Here are some of them in no particular order. If you have high levels of credit card debt, you might be making these already:

1. Minimum only payments - The way these are packaged and marketed sounds pleasing. 'Minimum payment' sounds as if the company is cutting you a deal. In fact, this is the interest only portion of the debt and your principal (the total amount you owe) is untouched. Making minimum only payments is a great way to remain in debt forever.
2. Paying late - Credit card companies earn a massive amount when you pay late. They effectively charge you

10 times the normal interest payment when you pay late.

3. Ignoring terms and conditions - Many credit cards offer introductory offers such as cash-back and cash bonuses to get people to sign on. This might lead you to think you're getting a great deal forever. Always check the full extent of the terms and conditions before signing up for one.

4. Not transferring balances - If you owe debt on multiple accounts, then you need to immediately consolidate this debt by transferring your balance to the card with the lower interest rate. If you don't do this, you'll be bleeding cash unnecessarily. Some cards have zero balance transfer fees so check with your bank about the terms on your cards.

TIPS TO REDUCE EXPENSES

As you've already learned, there are two sides to the budgeting equation. The first is to reduce your expenses and the second is to increase your income. You're now going to learn a few handy tips to reduce your expenses.

Explore Free Options

You're in school (or college). There's literally no other time in your life when people will lineup to give you free money, trust me! There are tons of websites that list scholarships that are available for you to apply to. Odds are good that you'll end up qualifying for one. Check out https://www.collegerank.net/best-scholarship-websites/ for a list of scholarship databases.

Another great resource are the counselors in your school or the admissions office of your college. Of course, you could get lied to like I was, but it never hurts to ask. Aside from free money, there are a number of ways you can reduce your spending on a bunch of other line items in your budget.

The first one that many students look for is free food. Campuses play host to a number of events that offer free food. Student unions often host international cultural events that serve food. Best of all, score a job in your university commons and you'll receive a free meal with every shift. High school students can take advantage of fairs and other events running in their local areas. Talk with your high school counselor, or a teacher.

Textbooks tend to be a common source of complaints when it comes to education. If you happen to be an upperclassman, see if you can get away with borrowing the book from your local or college library. Some students make photocopies of textbooks but this is a risky thing to do and you might find yourself slapped with a copyright violation (Tsay, 2020).

Check out websites such a BookBoon, OpenStax and Saylor Academy that offer free textbooks for college courses. While not every single textbook prescribed will be available, odds are good that you'll find some of the more commonly used text-books there.

Use Coupons or Cook at Home

If you're not a coupon hound as yet, what are you waiting for? These will reduce your expenses on groceries and other items drastically. On many campuses, producing your college ID card will ensure that you receive big discounts so use these for clothing purchases or for groceries.

Speaking of groceries, eat in the student dining halls or cook at home. Purchasing a meal plan and using it will result in a 25% discount over regular meal prices at most colleges. Cooking at home by preparing your meals ahead of time and buying groceries in bulk is a great way to learn a life skill as well as save money.

If you love your coffee, make your own. Buy beans in bulk and carry your coffee in a travel mug instead of spending over $3 per cup.

Living Expenses for College

College dorm accommodation is almost always more expensive than off-campus housing. Typically, it is the norm to live in dorms for a year before moving off campus into an apartment with your friends. It might be tempting to reduce your rental expenses completely, but keep your comfort in mind as well. Invest in a good bed and mattress so that you get good quality sleep instead of buying an airbed and trying to make do with that.

On the other hand, limit expenses that don't give you too much value. The idea of buying a huge flat screen TV might sound appealing to you but is it really something you need or can afford? Budget wisely and allocate these expenses accordingly.

Take advantage of deals that are offered around campus. Use resources such as Craigslist or ask your classmates for cheap housing deals. It might be a good idea to become an RA (Resident Assistant). RAs normally live in the dorms for free and typically need to undergo an orientation and training process.

Mind you there will be responsibilities you'll need to fulfill as part of this job, most of which will involve dealing with freshman shenanigans. However, the money you save on housing could go a long way towards helping you save money. Keep in mind that these accommodations don't come equipped with kitchens so you might have to increase your grocery budget by eating out or invest in a simple hot plate and microwave which limits your cooking options.

Entertain Wisely

Entertainment tends to be a huge expense item for most students. New-found freedom typically leads to all kinds of questionable purchases. There are some great ways to score free sources of entertainment when you're in school or in college.

For instance, if you live close to a big city, there may be many different choices for you to explore. A great option is to join a club. While the club might require membership dues, they offer a great way for you to expand your social circle and discover new ways to entertain yourself.

That being said, don't restrict yourself to free entertainment all the time. This just builds a mindset that you're poor. Instead, set yourself a budget that you can afford and then find options within it. You might find that some options are out of your reach but that many others are quite affordable.

Ask for Help

You're still in school (or college) and are not expected to be a financial expert. With this in mind, every educational institution has advisors who are ready to help you with your finances and to help you make better financial choices. Check with your school's student wellness center about the facilities available to you. If you're in high school, talk to your parents or adults you trust about money and finances.

Some students are hesitant to ask for help because they feel that they ought to have this whole finance and budgeting thing figured out. This is not the case at all. There are many working professionals out there who don't fully grasp the nuances of budgeting, so expecting a person in high school or college to master this is unrealistic.

Use the resources available to you. After all, this is literally what being resourceful means!

BUDGETING APPS

There are many apps out there that help you with creating a budget. However, the best one hands down is Mint. Mint was one of the first budgeting apps and began life as a website. The app seamlessly connects to your bank accounts and credit cards and categorizes your expenses easily.

You can also program your bill payment dates and receive alerts. Once you expand your wealth, it connects to your brokerage and retirement accounts as well. The app also provides you with your real-time credit score which is a huge plus. All in all, it's a great way to receive a snapshot of your financial situation. Mint also provides you with helpful advice and hints to help you make better sense of your budget.

If you have a problem staying disciplined with your budget, the app You Need a Budget (YNAB) is the best choice for you. YNAB is designed around helping people live with the money they actually have. This means every single dollar is accounted for and the app lets you create expense items only within this limit.

Mint, in contrast, allows you to float limits and doesn't do anything beyond highlight that line item in red. If you have debts to pay down and haven't consolidated them, YNAB will help you maximize the repayment schedule in an efficient way.

The YNAB app is paid, but the company reports that its users save $600 on average in the first month (Hong, 2019). This indicates that not only is the app useful, but users who struggle with budgeting discipline are well served here.

Lastly, if you love categorizing your expenses and don't want to give apps access to your bank accounts, you can try Wally. This is a free app where you can upload pictures of your receipts to enable the app to enter expenses directly. In other words, you don't need to enter anything manually.

Wally also has the option of allowing geolocation so you can categorize your expenditures by location as well. There are other apps, such as Acorns, that allow you to round your expenses to the nearest dollar and invest that change into a low-cost ETF. However, these apps fall into the making money category and aren't strictly about budgeting.

You'll learn more about investing apps later in the book. For now, let's move on and look at how you can put a stop to a huge hurdle that loses almost everyone money.

3

ENDING IMPULSIVE BUYING

D o you buy with your head or your emotions? This is a question that has bothered salespeople and marketers for a long time. Anecdotal evidence from salespeople always suggested that consumers buy with emotions and then create reasons to justify their behavior.

However, until recently this could not be proven as a fact. As a result, a lot of marketing theory and sales theory centered around appealing to the rational side of a consumer. Describing the benefits and listing how the product was superior and so on. The advent of social media advertising changed all of that. Marketing has now become a far more exact science and researchers have finally concluded what sales people always knew.

. . .

The fact is we have deep-seated emotions that drive us to purchase the things that we do. The root of these emotions is not relevant, from a marketing perspective, as much as it is important to elicit them. For example, you bought this book once you looked at the cover and the title. You looked at the table of contents and thought that this book might help you save money and avoid excessive debt.

These emotions stir certain memories within you and this what got you to reach out for this book instead of something else. The 'saving money and avoiding six figure debt part' becomes a rational justification that fits the emotion that is generated within you.

This is why brand name products are desired by consumers. They are largely seen as likeable and what's more, they trigger the herd mentality within all of us. The herd mentality, where we feel the need to imitate what others around us are doing, is a powerful psychological bias that most of us find difficult to ignore (Murray, 2020). In high school, this is also called peer pressure. You'll learn more about this later in this book.

Impulsive buying is something that can derail your hopes of saving money really quick. The ease with which one can shop online, for example, motivates impulsive buying. One thing you must understand is that avoiding situations where you're likely to break your discipline is far easier than having to refill the money spent. Think of it this way, money not spent is earning that same amount of money, and maybe more if you consider compounding interest as explained in chapter 1.

UNDERSTANDING IMPULSIVE BUYING

Numerous marketing studies indicate that impulsive buying occurs when our brains are primed to move away from their rational base. What does this mean? To understand this, we need to delve into psychology a bit more. Our brains have two parts to them. The first is the limbic system and the second is the prefrontal cortex or PFC.

The limbic system is found in almost every animal on earth and is the brain that first evolved within human beings. Think of how an animal makes decisions. Its needs are primal and it moves as and when these needs arise. It sees food, it moves to eat the food. It sees a predator and it runs.

There's no thinking involved here. Our limbic brains have the same effect on us when it comes to questions of survival. When you touch a hot object, you withdraw your hand instantly. You don't need to be told twice that holding onto a hot object will harm you. You go out of your way to avoid it once you've learned your lesson.

The negative experience is what drilled this into you. The emotions that it generated was so strong that it wired itself deeply into your brain and now, whenever someone comes at you with a hot object, you run the other way without thinking twice. Positive emotions associated with buying and spending work the same way.

The PFC on the other hand is the more evolved brain. It allows us to make considered decisions and think about them before carrying them out. The PFC is a slow mover but by taking the time to consider all options, it ends up making the right decisions for us. Generally speaking, the PFC is the better choice when it comes to making decisions that are best made rationally.

The problem is that the PFC is not the part of our brain that is automatically in charge. Because of its slow nature, it takes time to warm up, so to speak. If we're relaxed and in a peaceful state of mind, this gives the PFC more time to come online and it allows us to make better decisions.

The limbic brain on the other hand jumps into action when we encounter situations that require immediate decision-making or when we feel as if we don't have the resources needed to make a considered decision. By resources, I'm talking about perceived resources.

For example, if you're hungry and decide to go shopping, you're more likely to buy that tasty looking Snickers bar that's kept by the checkout. It costs just a couple of bucks and it's pretty tasty. It also fills you up reasonably well and it's a quick snack. At that point, your brain perceives that you're under stress (hunger) and therefore it is primed to activate the limbic system.

The minute it recognizes that you need to make a decision, it is the limbic system that comes online. Much like an animal that simply eats when it's hungry, you grab the bar of chocolate without concern for the future. As much as living in the present is a great thing, in this particular case it's safe to say that it isn't very helpful!

You can see the problem here. Since the limbic system is automatic, you have almost no chance of controlling how you react. This doesn't mean to say it's impossible. It's just that it's incredibly difficult to overcome millennia of evolution, which is what your limbic system is.

Studies have shown that we tend to make the worst long-term decisions when we're stressed or under some kind of emotional duress (Heshmat, 2020). Hunger is an example of an event that causes stress. Have you ever felt your brain shutting down because you're too hungry? You must have experienced how you have little patience for anything and simply want things to just sort themselves out.

Understanding your triggers and avoiding the situation is the best way forward. Studies indicate that men, on average, tend to overspend on electronic upgrades while women tend to spend unwisely on fashion and self-care products. This doesn't mean that every single man or woman conforms to this. It's the average behavior.

. . .

Ask yourself what are the times when you're moved to spend more than what you can afford? Which scenarios tend to get you overexcited? If you browse electronics online, do you find yourself losing all sense of proportion? You might say that you can't help it and feel the need to have to buy something!

This is biologically true when you're in the moment. However, you have full control of creating a disciplined framework within which you can control your behavior. You can choose to not go online. You can choose to unsubscribe to sale alerts and other prompts that encourage you to spend money that you don't have.

Do you have credit card information that is stored in your favorite online shopping portal for one-click checkout? Delete this information now! Another habit you can develop is to look at the cash in your wallet and imagine paying this amount when you place an order. Visualize holding the cash in your hand and physically handing it over to someone.

You are also in full control of creating a list of needs versus wants. You can pin this list somewhere visible and every time you want to buy something on impulse, you can refer to the list to check whether you're buying something you need or if you have enough space to spend on a want.

Most people don't create behavioral frameworks for themselves because it feels like too much work. They want the rush of dopamine that spending brings. This is why it's important to carry out the steps in the previous chapter and figure out how you can get your dopamine fix without having to spend money unnecessarily.

Remember that you always have a choice when it comes to spending. Stop trying to overcome your limbic system and instead, remove all situations that might exist to activate it instead. Think of it this way: If you want to be safe, would you try to cross the freeway on foot? You'd simply avoid walking anywhere close to it!

TIPS TO CURB IMPULSIVE BUYING

How should you go about creating a scenario where you don't need to worry about spending impulsively? Understand that despite all the preparation you'll undertake, you will be faced with scenarios where you'll be tempted to spend impulsively. These moments require willpower to overcome.

What you don't want to do is rely solely on willpower, as you've probably been doing so far. Willpower is meant to be used in short bursts. It isn't meant to be used to change large behavioral patterns. You need the PFCs help to overcome those challenges. This is what a framework does.

Do the Work

There's no shortcut here. You need to sit down and do everything that I've mentioned so far. You need to list your needs and wants, list the situations that move you into a stressed or emotional state, and make plans that counter them. Do you have a long stretch of classes between 10 A.M to 2 P.M, which leaves you exhausted at the end of it? High school classes will take up the majority of your day. If you decide to skip meals from the cafeteria, do you have a backup plan?

Does this cause you to go the nearest Subway and order a foot long with everything extra on it? You won't be able to unpack a full lunch and eat it in class, so cooking ahead of time and packing your lunch to go isn't going to work here. Instead, why not carry a handful of nuts or trail mix?

If you're a cereal hound, why not carry a little in a pouch and munch on it when you get the chance. Peanuts are a great choice for a healthy snack. You could technically pack bars or chocolate or one of those protein bars but remember that your health is important. These foods contain a lot of sugar so you need to eat healthy options.

Become aware of what your hunger signs are. Do you become slightly irritable when hunger begins to strike? Does your body undergo physical sensations, such as your stomach rumbling, head hurting and so on? Observe them and become aware.

Which other situations could you avoid entirely? For example, do you work at the local mall or shopping complex where there's a Gamestop next to your workplace? Do you often go in there and hangout with the employees and end up buying something?

How about changing your workplace entirely? Can you get a job that doesn't have any money spending temptations? Many types of jobs are available for you to consider. Working as a lab monitor or in a library is a great option.

Switch to Cash

If you're having problems curbing your spending then you have no earthly business hanging onto a credit card. You won't have one if you're in high school but remember this advice when you do get the chance to apply for one! Stick to a debit card or, even better, switch entirely to cash. These days large parts of the world are moving to digital payments so this might be tough but cash is still accepted almost everywhere.

Once you set your budget, figure out your weekly expenditure on necessities such as food, entertainment and travel. Withdraw that amount as cash and place it in your wallet and spend only this cash. You can use your debit card for emergencies. Forcing yourself to use cash will open your eyes to how much you're spending (and saving).

There is also the psychological effect of handing cash over that will make you think twice about buying something unnecessarily. Keep this habit up for six months and you'll marvel at how good you become at curbing unnecessary spending. Doing this will require some preparation.

The first thing to do is to separate your cash into different envelopes. You create one for food, another for entertainment and so on. Choose which categories you can switch to cash and create envelopes for them. Place the cash you will spend over a month into these envelopes. It might be better to first place weekly amounts since the last thing you want is to lose an envelope. Once you get used to spending from the envelopes, place monthly amounts in them. You'll also need to create a tracking system for these expenses.

Since you're spending cash, you might find that your online and offline worlds clash. If needed, create two separate tracking systems. If you use an app like Mint, you'll see the cash withdrawal show up under miscellaneous or uncategorized buckets. What you can then do is break this amount down into its respective components.

You'll have to do this manually of course but it's worth taking the time to do it. Make it a habit of doing this daily and you'll train your brain to become more conscious of how your money is being spent.

You will also need discipline. A common occurrence is people running out of cash before the month ends. You might have estimated your amount incorrectly or you might have overspent by mistake. To avoid a dilemma, you can create a tolerance zone for yourself. A tolerance zone is a predefined limit by which you're allowing yourself to exceed your spending limits.

Be careful with these. Do not think of these tolerance limits as being part of the limit. They only exist to account for your mistakes. Use these limits for the first two months and then stop. You should have a good handle on how much you spend after this period of time.

Watch Entertainment Expenses

What's the first thing you do with your friends after you've been out for a while? You probably head over the local greasy spoon, ice cream parlor or pizza joint and gorge yourself on something unhealthy. The problem with this behavior is that there are social repercussions to it.

You cannot sit there munching peanuts when everyone else is having pizza. The owner might not take kindly to this. Starving yourself is also not an option unless you're in a drastically bad place. If this is the case, you need to focus on making money a lot more than saving it.

Either way, starving yourself should never be an option. So, how do you handle this? One way is to account for it and allocate money towards it. It can be your weekly treat or one half of a weekly treat. If you know it's going to happen, don't fight it. If you enjoy these moments, as almost everyone does, go ahead and indulge yourself - but in a disciplined manner.

Instead, accept it as a part of your life and figure out how you can make room for it. You might have to curb your spending elsewhere. If you find that there are many of these 'necessary spending' items, you need to cut them off at some point and ask yourself how much of a need these really are. What is your spending threshold beyond which you will cut your wants out? Fix a limit in financial terms and stick to it.

Meanwhile, focus on making money once you've decided how much to cut. Cutting your expenses works best when you have a good level of income coming in. This is what allows you to become free. Neither side of the equation helps all by itself. It is only when you combine making money with cutting expenses that budgeting and 'saving' money works its magic.

Invest

You might not have the cash to invest in stocks or other financial instruments that grow your money. However, you can always invest in yourself. You're in school/college after all so why not use this opportunity to learn new skills or new ways of thinking that will make you a better person.

Don't view skills purely from a vocational perspective, although that helps. You need a steady dose of humanities along with practical skills. Your skills will be useless if you don't understand how to think critically. So, take a look at the courses being offered or ones that you can learn online outside of school hours and see which ones appeal to you the most.

Investing in yourself doesn't mean a formal education. For example, quality, well-researched books are the best source of knowledge; make it a habit to read as much as possible. Make time for it. If you have trouble staying focused when reading, start with short pieces or articles, and then expand your practice time to include longer reading sessions.

The more you invest in bettering yourself, the more you'll realize the true meaning of a need versus a want. You might even find some things that you felt were needs, were actually wants. This is how learning happens and you'll also gain better control over yourself and your habits.

Then there's the fact that you can learn new skills by investing in yourself that can boost your income levels. The more money you earn, the less stressed you'll be and your decisions will get better. So, make it a habit to better yourself. You'll find that your life will simply become a lot easier.

Apps and Memberships to Run Away From

Something that will go a long way towards curbing impulsivity is deleting your food ordering apps and other alerts that encourage you to spend money on stuff you don't need. If you've made the decision to cook food at home, which you should, then you don't really need these apps, for instance.

You'll probably allocate a single meal per week to eat out and to do this; you don't need to download or install an app. These apps are businesses and their objective is to manipulate you to spend as much money as possible. Their messaging and market is geared towards this and it isn't a surprise that you succumb to it.

Therefore, the thing to do is to eliminate them completely instead of trying to overcome the messaging. Don't sign up for memberships to these sites. Instead, invest that money in a membership at a wholesale grocery store and buy your food in bulk. Learn how to cook and you'll find that your health will improve massively because you won't be eating processed food anymore. You can even use YouTube and Pinterest to look for great recipes and learn how to cook instead of using them solely for entertainment purposes!

If you don't have time to go shopping for groceries, order them online and have them delivered. Alternatively, you can pick them up curbside. If you do have to install an app, install one that helps you figure out how to live better instead of an app that encourages you to spend money you don't have. High school students might not have to go grocery shopping but you'll do well to take note of this advice when you reach college.

Another source of needless expenditure are games that contain a ton of in-game purchases. The individual token that you need to buy might be inexpensive, but they add up pretty quickly. Games are designed to make you feel the need to keep coming back and, as a result, you'll end up spending a lot of money before you know it!

Install a productivity app such as Freedom or Stayfocusd. They do a lot more than just block websites. You can install time-based browsing controls as well as whitelist, or allow, certain websites.

Another great feature is that these programs also block any apps on your computer that can cause a distraction when you're studying. Fortnite and Outlook and so on get automatically blocked so that you can focus on what's important.

Manage Cards

I've already mentioned how to get rid of credit cards and that you're best off without one. You need to be smart about how you take care of this, though. Calling the bank and asking them to cancel your account is not a smart thing to do. This is because shutting down a credit account can hurt your credit score and this will hurt your financial future.

Instead, what you need to do is physically destroy your cards and limit the number of things you spend on them. Here's a good way to do this. Pick one card and choose one payment that can be made on it. For example, you can automate your phone bill's payment on this card or your Netflix. If you choose to not automate payment, record the card's number and other information someplace safe.

Now, cut up your cards and dispose of them. You don't need the physical card anymore. As long as you have the number or have automated a small bill payment on it, you'll be just fine. This way, it'll be physically impossible for you to spend anything on your credit card.

Why should you do it this way? First, paying bills on time helps build your credit score. Credit bureaus take your overall borrowing limit into account when determining this. Let's say you have four cards with a limit of $10,000 each. This gives you a total limit of $40,000.

Now let's say you have a $50 outstanding balance that can still be paid off in the grace period. This $50 debt represents 0.12% of your overall borrowing ability. The credit bureau reads this as you borrowing a small amount of your capacity and deems this a good thing.

Now let's say that you call the bank and ask them to cancel three cards. Your overall limit is now $10,000 and you've borrowed $50 against this limit. This is 0.5% of your overall limit. In other words, your borrowing has jumped almost four times. The credit bureau doesn't see the elimination of lines of credit as a good thing. Instead, it only calculates the proportion of the total limit you've borrowed and assigns you a credit score accordingly. Someone who borrows 0.12% has a better score than someone who borrows 0.5%. This doesn't mean to say that a person who borrows the latter proportion automatically receives a poor score.

It's just that you need to be careful about cancelling credit card accounts. If you're close to the limit on one card, then cancelling the others might be the worst thing for you to do. Your borrowing percentage will zoom close to 100% and your credit score will drop like a rock.

. . .

Keep your accounts open until you've cleared all balances and when your recurring spend on it is a very small proportion of your overall limit. In the example I just highlighted, you can get away with cancelling your credit cards since 0.5% is still a very small proportion of your limit.

Shop for Clothes Wisely

Guys have it relatively easier here. There aren't that many options for men's clothes and it's pretty easy to buy four t-shirts, two shirts and a couple of jeans, shorts and slacks, and they're good to go. Us girls have it tougher, but it's possible. The thing to do is to view it as a challenge!

Buy 14 pieces of clothing that you can mix and match together to create a new outfit. For example, if you buy seven tops and seven bottoms, this gives you 49 outfits to wear. That's more than one and a half months' worth of outfits!

Clothes shouldn't be a problem for you if you shop for them smartly!

One of the biggest triggers of impulsive buying is the peer pressure that is formed on social media. This is a big problem to deal with and it deserves its own chapter.

4

DEFEAT THE PRESSURE TO SPEND

D id you hear the story of how that one guy dropped six grand on his birthday at the club? Well, not only did I hear about it, I lived it! One of my friends decided to take his shiny new credit card along with him and left his tab open at a club in Miami Beach. The bill totaled six grand, and he confessed to having no idea how he managed to spend that much! But hey, he did manage to capture some sweet selfies!

This kind of thing happens alarmingly often and it's easy to laugh at the person and think that you'll never be that irresponsible. Well, guess what? You're being that irresponsible every single day! Social media is a non-stop validation train and, for all the good it does, it also has the ability to bring out the worst in us.

· · ·

Aside from lowering the standard of debate drastically, social media also encourages us to chase things that are not important for us in any way at all. All platforms are pretty smart now, and they've figured out how to keep you engaged by showing you content that you'll love.

Every move of yours on the platform is scrutinized and feeds the algorithm information about what you love to consume. This in turn feeds the validation centers of your brain as you go deeper and deeper into engaging with the platform. Soon, the validation you receive through social media will become irresistible and the next thing you know, you're living for it.

This isn't just what happens with people who post regularly on social media, by the way. Even if you are a lurker, the same cycle happens. You constantly view content that satisfies you and justifies your view of things and you lose the ability to remain impartial. In short, you lose perspective and once you're in it, it can be hard to extricate yourself.

Withdrawing from social media can feel a lot like quitting tobacco or alcohol for someone who is deeply addicted to it. This is biologically true. Researchers at Harvard determined that social media consumption lights up the same centers of the brain as addictive substances ("Social Media Addiction," 2020). No wonder the withdrawal symptoms are similar!

You've already read about dopamine and the role it plays. Receiving a "like" or a comment brings validation that releases dopamine into your brain and soon it becomes addictive. Social media also warps the way we look at ourselves. Our brain's reward centers tend to light up when we talk about ourselves.

In real life conversations, you can't get away with focusing on yourself all the time. Researchers estimate that people do this around 40% of the time in physical interactions.

However, social media conversations are not real conversations. It's just one person talking about themselves and then another talking about themselves and each validating their own point of view without taking the others' into consideration. On social media, people end up talking about themselves close to 90% of the time ("Social Media Addiction," 2020). Is it any wonder that we keep going back?

The continuous reward system of social media gets people to keep going back to it, and they begin to rely on it for relief from anxiety and other problems.

SOCIAL MEDIA AND SELF ESTEEM

Research has shown that there is a strong link between excessive social media use and mental states of depression, anxiety and poor self-esteem. The rewards that "likes" and comments on your content leads to a sort of dependence on them. Next thing you know, you're living for them.

·   ·   ·

This creates pressure to develop content that brings even more likes and at this point, you're well down the rabbit hole. Another danger of excessive social media use is that it leads to comparing the material things one has. American culture is pretty materialistic to begin with.

Music and pop culture is full of people flashing their cash and jewels and wearing the latest designer stuff that no one needs. Everyone is perfect in every way possible. This is magnified on social media. The girl next door morphs into a supermodel with over 500,000 followers. The biggest proof that she is an influencer is that she follows just 500 people in return!

You look at her and want what she has and this encourages you to buy the clothes she has, the shoes she has and so on. That's how you're also going to get the type of guy she has in her life (who has his typically adventurous profile where he's back flipping off things, of course!).

The platform itself pushes this type of content to manipulate you to stay on for longer. You begin to think that if you don't start working toward this goal, you're going to miss out. The fear of missing out, or FOMO, is one of those primal instincts that motivates us to do a lot of things.

Social media amplifies and exaggerates it to ridiculous levels. This is partly because our expectations and thoughts when on the platform are also ridiculous. Studies indicate that the less you know someone in real life, the more you're going to believe that they're happier and more successful than you.

None of this does your self-esteem any good. Human beings have an inbuilt tendency to compare themselves to others irrationally, to begin with. We compare every little imperfection of our own with the perfect image we see in others. Another way to think of this is to say that we compare our feature length movies with their trailers. There's no way we can ever come off best in this.

When we migrate this behavior to social media, we're comparing every single one of our imperfections to how we perceive others to be. This is how anxiety and depression is triggered. If you spend more than three hours per day on social media, odds are good that you're at risk.

Herd Mentality

Why does FOMO arise in the first place? Why is it such a powerful pull? The answer lies in the fact that there is a deeper bias that drives this and many other fears. This bias is commonly referred to as the herd mentality. If you've ever seen a flock of sheep in real life, you'll know what this is.

Sheep stick together no matter what. They'll go where every other sheep is going and will never push back against an instruction. This is how a single dog or person can control a large herd of them. As much as we laugh at sheep, human beings can be startlingly similar.

The herd mentality ties in with our survival instinct. If you find yourself in an unfamiliar place or country where you don't speak the language, what are you going to do? You'll look around and simply do what everyone else is doing. There's safety in numbers after all.

This is why we form societies and communities and react strongly when someone challenges this norm. The more of a struggle life is, the more a person is expected to conform to what everyone else is doing. The herd mentality causes us to do many things we don't necessarily need or want to do.

Even worse, it convinces us that doing these things would be good for us and it helps us overcome our rational thoughts. Social media takes this herd mentality and dials it up to ridiculously high levels. You see someone posing on a mountain top and the next thing you know, you're booking your tickets to go do the same thing.

The bad news is that there is no way for you to completely eliminate your herd mentality bias. It allows you to survive and switching it off would be detrimental to you. However, you can bring it back to healthy levels by disciplining your social media usage. You have a natural tendency to want to hang with the cool kids and social media uses this to the extreme.

It takes this tendency and warps your definition of cool and gets you to believe things that have nothing to do with you. You might create the best budget and have strict spending limits but when you're asked to go to that amazing music festival where everyone was taking selfies at yesterday, you can't resist.

Next thing you know you've blown a month's worth of entertainment money in a single night. The question is, how do you curb this sort of behavior? The method itself is pretty straightforward. What's tough is implementing it. This is because social media usage triggers the most primal centers of our brain.

Primal in this sense refers to our limbic system that we talked about earlier. You'll end up acting automatically since the gratification and validation will trigger your pleasure centers that are tied to your survival instincts. Once they're removed, or if they disappear, you're pushed into survival mode and the limbic system takes over completely.

It isn't just the herd mentality that plays a role in getting you to overspend. Once you do spend too much, optimism helps you justify it. You might simply feel that you'll always make more money in the future and that the current gratification that you're receiving is justified. In short, you borrow from the future.

The problem is that you have no way of knowing how the future is going to play out. No one can ever predict the future. You can't even predict the next minute so relying on some phantom income from the future doesn't make much sense. What's really happening here is that the herd mentality is pushing you into making bad decisions and locking it with optimism.

So, not only are you making a poor financial decision, you're also feeling good about it - at least temporarily! You might be misled into thinking that sitting at home and doing nothing is the best course of action but this is not the case at all. That's the other extreme, which you need to avoid as well.

If there's one tenet you should adopt when it comes to your financial life, it is to strike balance between everything. Living at the extremes is not a good choice since you'll be dealing with the unexpected there. Instead, find a healthy balance. Yes, you'll make mistakes and this is a part of life and the trial and error process.

Finding a balance also requires you to have conversations with your friends about spending money. You don't need to disclose your precarious position to them. Instead, tell them that you're saving up for a new car or an apartment or something else. If they're true friends, they'll understand and will cut back with you. Besides, they're probably under the same pressure as you are and may appreciate you bringing up a solution!

Stay away from people who pressure you to spend money unnecessarily or encourage you to repeatedly violate your discipline. It sounds trite to say this, but you need to cut such people out of your life. They'll typically bring you nothing but grief.

Instead of going out to a fancy club and ordering drinks, why not enjoy a matinée movie and split a tub of popcorn?

Most importantly, develop a discipline around your social media usage. Disable notifications from social media like Facebook, Twitter and Instagram. These platforms are generally not used to communicate with anyone in your immediate social circle anyway, so there's no reason you need to have them actively open.

Keep your messaging apps open and reduce your consumption of garbage in the media. I'm not saying you should be ignorant, but stop dedicating so much mental energy to things that don't matter to you.

STOPPING FOMO AND DEVELOPING A SCORECARD

The billionaire investor and philanthropist Warren Buffett has said a lot of things about investing wisely and about evaluating a business. One of the most important things he's spoken about is the phenomenon of being an inner scorecard person. Buffett made this comment in the context of speaking about his father (Schroeder, 2009).

He mentioned that from a young age, he noticed that his father Howard didn't really bother too much with the opinions of other people. He stuck to his guns and asserted his opinion no matter what. Warren was smart enough to realize that his father often took this tendency to an extreme, and it cost him quite a lot.

However, the point about relying on the inner scorecard is relevant. Deriving gratification and satisfaction from the things within you, instead of outside of you, is what will put you on the path to satisfaction. This makes sense when you think about it logically.

You can never control what someone else thinks of you. No matter what you do, no matter how good your actions are, there will always be someone who will not be fond of you. There's no controlling this. Basing your sense of self-esteem on what others think is a lot like building a home on ground that is constantly shifting in an earthquake.

People's opinions change all the time and you can't control this, either. Nor can you predict it. It's far easier to ask yourself what's important to you and to those you truly care about.

Act according to those standards. The beauty of this approach is that our loved ones typically accept us unconditionally and have some pretty easy standards to achieve. Your mom doesn't care that you have the latest designer handbag or the best VR gear. All she wants is for you to be a good person and to be happy.

It's easy to be a good person and being happy is connected to this. How convenient! So, become an inner scorecard person instead of an outer scorecard one. Your life will end up being a lot simpler and you'll be more grounded. Comparing yourself to others leads to all of the negatives I've mentioned already.

When you stop comparing yourself to those around you, whether in real life or in social media, you'll end up creating some huge benefits for yourself.

You'll Stop Believing Lies

Almost everyone knows this by now and yet it bears repeating: Social media content is a lie! It does not reflect the real lives of the people behind it. The problem is that despite knowing this, you'll end up believing the lies to a certain extent if you keep exposing yourself to it.

Most of your favorite social media accounts have beautiful and perfect-looking people representing a business. Celebrities who post mirror selfies with some over-priced facial cream or product are consciously trying to manipulate you to buy what they are promoting. It is their job to represent the brand they are advertising. Even the allegedly candid moments are all scripted, everything we see is calculated to create motivation, so we can spend more money. Some celebrities probably don't even care about their followers as much as they say they do. They, themselves, and/or their media management team over-state their devotion to followers because they have a purpose, to influence our behaviour.

Ask yourself whether you like being used in this way. What if someone behaves this way in real life? Would you give them even a second glance? Of course not! Yet, somehow all of this is okay on social media.

Stop being used in this way. Once you do this and reduce your social media consumption, you'll find that your brain will be more relaxed and that you won't find yourself constantly worrying about what others think of you.

Get a Better Understanding of What Success is

The "celebrities" on social media, aside from being slightly deceptive about their true life, also have a ton of support staff whose sole job it is to make them look great. They have access to a nutritionist, a fitness trainer, a chef, a skin care expert, a brand manager, a publicist and an army of workers who make sure their every little need is taken care of.

It's no wonder that they can post non-photoshopped images of themselves looking pristine. It's easy to take a look at this and develop warped ideas of what perfection looks like or that achieving this is equivalent to success. The fact is that not everyone is born with equal advantages.

There are some people who are born rich and with unbelievably good genes. This is perfectly fine and has nothing to do with you. Most of the time, that lucky person is looking at someone else and envying their lives. There will always be someone who looks better than you, who's richer than you and does more things than you.

If you stay away from social media, you'll realize that none of this affects your life in any way. After all, it's their life and unless you know them personally, you're unlikely to be affected. Social media however warps reality and gets you to believe that you need to measure up to what is going on out there.

It gets you to compare your life with someone else's despite both of your circumstances being completely different. If you knew them in real life, you'd recognize that they've had massive assistance in projecting who they are. You don't get to see any of that online.

However, you certainly can control your exposure to these lies in the first place. There's no rule that says you have to be present on some platform all the time. You can switch them off and get on with your life and define real goals that bring you success. Remember that the definition of success depends on what's important to you.

Define what your standards are and work to hit them. Don't rely on social media or any hysterical media source to tell you what your standards ought to be.

True Motivation

In real life, true motivation comes from within. You look at someone who's working out in the gym and sweating profusely, you're not thinking about the likes he gets on his Instagram. Instead, you're looking at how hard he works and how much he pushes himself. Your desire is to emulate those qualities.

I'm not saying that people don't seek validation from real life sources. It's just that it's a bit harder to do this as compared to social media. Visit anyone's profile and the first thing you prominently see is someone's social proof. For example, you clearly see the number of followers when visiting someone's Instagram page.

You clearly see the retweets and likes on a Facebook post. This is intentional. Social proof numbers activate your herd mentality instinct and you end up engaging with that content even more. Comparing yourself to others is the primary means of engagement on social media.

So, disconnect from it and reduce your consumption of it. If you can manage it, try a detox for a week or two. There's no need to go to the other extreme and vilify it as being completely evil. There is a lot of good to be found in social media, it's just that you need to create a balance with it.

In terms of spending, decreasing your social media consumption will lead to healthier spending habits. I'm not making this up! According to research carried out by the National Bureau of Economic Research, social media use and irresponsible spending patterns are correlated (Ingraham, 2017).

When engaging in social media, we're no longer trying to keep up with just the Joneses, we're also competing with the thousands of Joneses from all around the world. This warps our thinking when it comes to what makes us happy and what counts as a reasonable purchase.

So, do yourself a favor and minimize social media in your life, use it for business or to make money. That way, you'll derive some value from it!

5

THE BEST BANG FOR YOUR BUCK

We take our lives for granted when we're kids. Our parents provide for us, and we don't spend a lot of time wondering about things like money or security. In fact, when we graduate high school we relish the chance at finally being 'free.' I know I certainly did!

However, living by yourself requires huge responsibility. Are you ready to truly live by yourself? In this chapter, let's begin looking at some tips to stretch your dollar when it comes to housing and food.

HOUSING

Aside from your tuition, housing costs will be your major expense in college. Once you step out into the real world, housing and food will be your biggest expenses. Learning good spending habits now, will pay off for the rest of your life.

Dorm life might scare you away from living with a roommate ever again, but it's the easiest way to save money. While you're stuck with a certain roommate in a dorm, this isn't the case when you move to off-campus housing where you can choose to room with like-minded people.

If your family lives close to campus, consider living with them for a while. In some areas, off-campus housing can be relatively expensive. This means you'll need to save money before you can afford a place. If you can live with your family for a bit longer, it will be a huge help in the long run. You'll save by doing this, just put any inconveniences in perspective!

Campuses are full of listings for places available for rent. However, it pays to network and ask around. There might be some rooming situation available that would suit you perfectly, for example. What's more, the landlord might be someone familiar to you, so this would be an added bonus.

Some students look at off-campus housing as a chance to finally live in a situation of their dreams and tend to go after the most desirable properties. But, these also tend to be the most expensive. Keep an open mind and look at areas that are more affordable and still safe.

.   .   .

Often, places that are a bit further away from campus will be cheaper to rent. You might have increased transportation costs, so look at all sides of the picture.

If you do find a great deal that's off-campus, consider investing in a cheap mode of transportation. Is there someone you can carpool with? How about buying a bicycle for yourself? You'll also manage to get some exercise in! Consider all options of transportation and see if you can develop a solution to make cheap housing work.

Believe it or not, there are even many campus affiliated senior centers that offer cheap housing to students. Check with your school's housing office to see if you can get in on this. For example, NYU offers its students free housing in senior centers around New York City. In a place like New York, that offer goes a long way!

I've already mentioned how becoming an RA can be a great gig to score cheap housing and get the university to pay for your living expenses. Another option is to become a property manager for the rental companies in your town. You'll have to coordinate activities and take care of the apartments, but will receive a small unit with a basic salary as compensation.

Keep in mind that this will be a full-time job and it might interfere with your study schedule. However, if you can make it work, it's a great option.

If you can manage it, see if you can score a deal living in an RV or some other mobile home. This tip is more practical in rural areas. Tiny houses or converted basement apartments may also be an option as a great way to score reduced housing costs.

Above all else keep your safety in mind when trying to score a great deal.

Remember to budget your expenses and track all of them. Make sure your estimates are in line with what you're spending. Learn to carry over expenses from one category to another. For example, you might spend more on food one week, but you can reduce your entertainment expenses by the amount you overspent.

You might overspend one month but you can cut back on the next. Keep accumulating as much money as you can to build an emergency fund and backup living expenses.

SCHOOL SUPPLIES

School supplies tend to eat up a significant amount of your budget. Here's how you can save money on them.

Use websites such as Valorebooks to rent your textbooks instead of buying them. Amazon and Chegg are also great sources for textbooks. You can also buy the e-book versions since these tend to be cheaper. The best solution of all would be to see if you could borrow them from someone who's finished the class or buy it from them.

Start saving up money well in advance of the next semester to avoid having to come up with cash on short notice to pay for your supplies. It's best to start with small goals. Aim to pay for at least one or two textbooks instead of having to ask your parents for money. Gradually increase your savings over time until you reach a point where you can pay for your supplies yourself.

Back-to-school-time is a great period to find bargains on tons of school supplies, especially the basic ones. Notebooks, pens, pencils can typically sell for huge discounts. Shop wisely and source the best deals for supplies.

There are many places you can buy school supplies cheaply such as The Dollar Store. Make sure you check Craigslist's free supplies section, as well, to see if you can score some great deals in supplies. You might find that furniture and other items such as notebooks might be given away by people for free.

The first week of college typically has many welcome-back events run by various associations on campus. Aside from the possibility of free food, you can also score other free stuff that is distributed at these events.

A left-field source of school supplies are career fairs. Whether you qualify for a job or not, talk to recruiters at these events. You'll usually end up scoring a few pens and other stationery for free. Head over to them with your resume and you might land a job as well!

If you live near a major metropolis, check to see if you can volunteer at these events. The companies that pitch here will offer you massive bags of goodies. If the event happens to be connected to your area of study, you can even get some handy networking done. Check the websites of popular convention centers and trade centers in your area for opportunities to volunteer.

Amazon has a robust student discount section where you can trade in laptops, textbooks and even get gift cards on purchases. You might even qualify for a free Amazon Prime membership. Recycle centers tend to be great sources of supplies. You can find great furniture, home decor and tons of other supplies for free. Art students will find that paint and other art supplies are often provided at recycling centers.

Your college may offer printing services for free; make use of this as much as possible. You're paying tuition, so it makes sense to use these resources as much as possible.

I've just spent an entire chapter railing against social media, but it helps to use social media to score free stuff. If you have an account that has a lot of followers you can use it to get samples or other products for free. You don't need to have huge fan followings to do this.

Depending on the brand you're aiming at, an account with even smaller levels of social reach will qualify. I'll address this more in the next chapter but it's something to keep in mind.

Check with your school to see if they offer any programs where students can qualify for a free laptop or computer. Stores around campus will offer students discounts so check these out as well. Another great way to score good deals is to buy refurbished laptops and computers from online retailers.

In addition to this, companies such as Freecycle offer used tech at fair prices. These tend to be a bit risky, but often they're worth the price.

Check to see if you and your roommates can save by opting for a bundled phone plan. Some phone companies offer them in certain locations. You can certainly save by opting for a bundled home internet and phone plan. These days, some companies even offer free laptops and tablets upon signing up.

A great way to make sure the life of your computer is extended, is to use cloud-based storage services as much as possible. For example, Google gives you 15 GB worth of free storage through its Google Drive product. External hard drives are also a good option, although they cost money and it's easy to lose them. However, you can use them to store older data and avoid using up all of your free 15 GB space in the cloud.

By having nothing stored locally, you can restore your PC to an earlier date, install a few updates, and you'll have a machine that's close to brand new. Make sure you back up all of your data, or even better, work directly on the cloud and don't use local software. Google also offers word processing, presentation and spreadsheet software for free.

If you do need sophisticated software, use the local computer lab or the department labs to do your work.

Black Friday, despite the uncivilized mayhem it promotes, will get you ridiculously good deals on technology. Or, wait for Cyber Monday and get these products delivered right to your doorstep.

Use your birthday. Create a wish list or a registry on websites such as Amazon. That way, if anyone asks you what you want as a gift, you can point them towards it. Consider asking people to contribute money towards something if those close to you can't afford the entire purchase.

Limit your home internet use as much as possible and reduce the cost of that plan. Instead, study in places with free Wi-Fi or use the college's resources as much as possible. This might not be practical at all times, but it is a good way to save on home internet bills. In case of emergency, you can use your phone as a hotspot to stream what you need.

Some companies offer free copies of their software if you sign up using an .edu address. Avast, Microsoft, OpenOffice are examples of such companies. While the offers vary, you can use them to your advantage. Another option is to take advantage of trial versions of software before deciding to purchase them. You'll need just an email address to sign up. Be careful, though. Some trial offers require you to enter credit card information, so that they can start billing you immediately when the trial is over. In that case, set a reminder on your calendar to cancel the subscription before you get charged.

ENTERTAINMENT

Entertainment is a pretty important part of student life, but it typically involves many expenses. Use these tips to reduce your spending on entertainment options. You'll find that money and fun aren't always as connected as you might think!

Your student ID is a powerful thing. Carry it with you wherever you go and you'll get discounts and other free stuff. Many outlets near and on campus offer discounts during selected hours so make full use of this.

Outdoor Options

Before heading out, eat something at home and then order an appetizer instead of a full meal at a restaurant. If dessert is your thing then order just that. Get together with your friends and use happy-hour discounts.

Many restaurants offer all-you-can-eat deals on Saturday afternoons. The same food is sold at almost triple the price for dinner. Go late in the afternoon and have a meal that carries you through until the next day.

If you are a movie buff and have to head to the theater, see if you can score cheaper tickets for matinée or late-night shows. These tend to attract smaller crowds and you can get better deals on these tickets.

Your local library or even a few student organizations might offer free movie screenings, so check out those listings as well. There is really no need to ever pay full-price for a movie.

When it comes to entertainment, Groupon is a huge boon for students everywhere. Typically, venues offer discounts for groups or even for individuals. Use these opportunities and make use of the offers on the website.

Joining a campus club or a student organization might be a great decision if your priority is frugal entertainment. These events will also offer you many chances to network; who knows where that might lead?

Many metropolitan areas have some pretty cool museums. Did you know that the Metropolitan Museum of Art, which is one of the most famous museums in the world, requires just a donation to enter? You can donate as little as $5 or if you're a student, you may get away with paying nothing at all.

Museums also have free-admission days to drum up publicity. They're also great places to work or volunteer. These places often host large fundraisers, and if you can score a job working at one of these events, you might just get the chance to take that selfie with your favorite celebrity, or just do some networking.

Even if you live in a major metropolitan area, there's usually a forest somewhere nearby. Join a local hiking club to explore the wilderness. Hiking only requires sturdy shoes and a backpack. Use sites like Meetup to either create your own group or join some for free.

Indoor Options

Use services such as Netflix, or borrow DVDs from your local library to get your movie fix on the weekend. These services typically require a one-time cost but you'll find that they are cheaper than traditional options. If you qualify for a free Amazon Prime membership, you can find some excellent movies on the platform for free.

While being prudent with your money at all times might not sound like the coolest thing to do, you and your friends can brainstorm ways to entertain yourselves. Board games are always a great option. Investing in a PS4 or an Xbox might be worth it if you're going to be living together for a while.

Try to be as frugal as possible with your entertainment and avoid spending too much money every single time you go out. You do need to have fun, but this doesn't mean you need to spend money every single weekend.

If you're a gamer, you probably have your entertainment settled, no matter what it looks like to the outside world. These days, gaming is a legitimate source of revenue where you can earn a bit of income in many ways. I'll cover this in more detail in the next chapter.

Lastly, we have good old YouTube. It seems possible to find the most obscure videos to enjoy for a break from your studies, and of course, it's mostly free.

For example, if you happen to be a football fan, did you know that the NFL posts old episodes of Hard Knocks on its channel? The league also has another channel where it posts classic games from both the playoffs and the regular season. Tons of sports leagues around the world do the same thing and you can spend countless hours entertaining yourself.

Keep in mind that you can change the settings within YouTube so that you're shown channels that appeal to you. You can filter your results to show you videos about educational topics. This will prevent you from rushing out and buying your favorite NFL player's jersey or spending money in some other way.

If this fails, there's always Reddit!

LET'S TALK ABOUT FOOD

Saying that food is the most important item in our lives is an understatement. Food is important and inevitable. Often times when we are too busy we forget to eat and that leads to snack hunting; searching for something, anything that could fill that void so we can keep moving. When we are hungry money does not matter and we could easily spend at least $10 in a fastfood restaurant. If this happens to you twice a week, you are actually spending $80 a month, money that could be used to feed you every day in that month.

In this part of the book, I want to help you avoid these scenarios, help you remember that meals cost money and time, and show you how you could manage both easily from home regardless of your circumstances. First and foremost, you will need to buy a rice cooker, or a crock-pot - No, this is not an expense, it is an investment that in the long term will help you save more money than the amount you spent on this (these) items - These cooking tools will make it easier to plan and cook healthy meals accordingly.

I highlighted an example previously where you might have a stretch of classes that prevent you from eating properly. Plan your eating schedule ahead of time. It really doesn't take that long. You can buy insulated lunch packs with ice packs in them. This will solve any need to find a fridge to store your meals when you're roaming around campus. And yes, they're available at the Dollar Store.

Set aside time beforehand to prep your food. Instead of cooking elaborate meals, design grab-and-go meals such as pre-prepared salads, wraps and sandwiches. These are easy to store and you can carry them with you wherever you go.

Another great resource for you to check out is YouTube and Pinterest. These are great sources of cheap and easy to cook meals; in the case of YouTube, you'll be able to follow along as the meal is cooked! In addition to this, local farmer's markets and flea markets have great deals on food. If you live by yourself, this is a great way to save money on groceries without having to depend on your parents for money.

While buying in-bulk does save you money, you'll need the containers and storage space for food items. Also, focus on getting everyday necessities in bulk, things like toilet paper household cleaners, soap, detergent and so on.

As for food, you can buy frozen food but keep in mind that some of these foods are heavily processed. While they might be cheap, you want to eat healthy as well.

You can split memberships to bulk buying stores, like Costco, with your roommates. If you have the same tastes in food, this makes a lot of sense. Then you can buy your food in bulk and both of you will save money on these purchases.

Keep an eye for coupons and special deals from retail outlets. Shop for the cheaper brands and buy generic brands as much as possible. Often, stores sell products that are their own brands and these tend to be cheaper.

Here's one way to score gourmet food. Walk into a Whole Foods, or any other higher end grocery store, and look for deals on food that is expiring soon. Be careful to consume the food before it expires. Often, eggs, yogurt, milk and even meat are sold like this.

The food in campus commons might not be the best tasting, but it sure will be cheap. As I mentioned earlier, buying in advance usually results in a 25% discount on food. If you can score a job there, you'll even get one meal per shift. Free food is always tasty!

Ramen by itself is decent but it can be made even better. Add some meat, spices and tofu and suddenly you're got yourself a gourmet meal. Look up recipes to cook ramen online and you'll see that they aren't complicated. They often (literally) boil down to throwing some cut vegetables into boiling water and then adding in the ramen at the end.

In the real world, happy hours are mostly associated with alcohol. But in college settings happy hour deals typically involve food. Keep an eye out for these deals and collect any relevant coupons. Split them with a friend and try to source the best deals possible!

Almost every place will give you, at least, free ice cream on your birthday. Look for birthday deals in eating joints around your campus. Combine this with your weekly treat and you'll earn double points!

Punch cards can be a double-edged sword. You need to spend money in order to earn the rewards it offers. The first thing to do is to check whether the card is worth it. For example, if you need to spend $8 buying food 10 times ($80) to earn a free meal worth $8, your effective price per meal is $7.20 (80 divided by 11.)

This is still pretty considerable. Work out what you usually spend and, if it's worth it, use a punch card. A better way to use this deal is to split the rewards with a friend. Let them buy half the punches and you buy the rest.

Your average price per meal will still be the same but the amount you spend will reduce so it might be worth it for you.

If you have a car and have signed up for AAA membership, did you know that you can earn discounts at select dining locations? There are many such perks that organizations offer so be sure to check all of them out. Student discounts are also offered at a variety of places, so do your research.

Services such as Imperfect Foods reduce the cost of buying groceries by as much as half. This company stocks food that is close to its expiry date or has been rejected by supermarket chains, for whatever reason. Currently, this is most common in California and Oregon, but there's no doubt you see this service as it expands.

If working in the school cafeteria isn't a good option for you, try scoring a job as a waiter or waitress or as a dishwasher in a restaurant. Typically, waiters and waitresses make money with tips, so the pay can be uneven and the job can be pretty stressful. But, there is often free food involved.

Depending on the business, you might get a free meal or heavily discounted prices on menu items. Another great option is to work in a grocery store. These stores typically give employees free samples as well as allow employees to take produce that has been rejected for whatever reason.

There are many programs such as food banks and SNAP benefits that provide food for low-income students. If you're really struggling, check out these resources and get the help you need.

Don't use credit cards! Have I mentioned this already? Use credit cards wisely, as detailed previously, and you'll build your credit history safely and avoid dangerous expenditures.

FASHION

Mix and match your existing clothes to come up with as many combinations as possible. Still need clothes? Try the thrift shop! If Macklemore can find enough stuff in there to look good, so can you!

Find that balance between needlessly paying for something and being overly thrifty. Use your birthday to score some fabulous deals. Shops like Sephora give you free gifts on your birthday if you're a member. In addition to this, they offer free samples of almost everything they stock!

GIGS WITH SAVING PERKS

I'll talk about making money in the next chapter in detail. For now, remember that you need to make money somehow or at the very least, find gigs that come with perks that help you save. You might be a student but this doesn't mean you can't earn money on the side. Work a campus job that gives you perks, work in some field you're interested in or volunteer somewhere in exchange for perks.

A good campus job, if you happen to live in a sports-mad college campus, is to be a game day vendor. You get to watch games for free and earn a huge amount of money in tips. Focus on the upper bleachers and you'll easily clear a few hundred every weekend over and above your hourly rate.

Teaching assistant jobs are also available for those who ask for them. Typically, these go to upperclassmen but it is possible for sophomores to be hired as TAs for freshman level courses. Perform well in a class and develop a relationship with the professor. If they have any openings, they'll let you know.

A paid internship is another option you should explore. If you happen to be studying in a technical field such as engineering, internships with companies will add huge value to your degree and will show potential employers that you're serious about learning skills. Best of all, if it's paid, you get to earn money while you learn!

DEALS, MEMBERSHIPS AND FREE STUFF

Need to find cheap furniture? Try Craigslist or look for notices on campus. Avoid spending on odds and ends as much as possible and source these for free as much as possible

Here's a neat trick. Did you know that there are companies that offer free samples of common household products like cleaners and toilet paper? The best known one is samplebuddy.com. You can also shop at the Dollar Store and other thrifty stores to pick up household goods on the cheap.

Done with that textbook? Sell it! If you have some clothes or other things that you don't want to use anymore, sell all of it. There will always be people who are on the lookout for stuff, so take advantage of this.

Apps such as Offerup and Letgo are quite popular when it comes to this, as well as Craigslist or Facebook Marketplace. You can go online and literally search 'free' or 'free stuff' on these websites and you'll find some great items that are being given away.

Scholarships

There are so many scholarships offered in the United States; the only people who don't qualify are either those who don't need it or international students. If you're looking for tuition assistance, chances are good that there is some program, somewhere, that will give you some assistance.

A great resource to find which scholarship is available to you is scholarship.com. In addition to this, you can also speak to counselors before you graduate high school to figure out which college is affordable and gives you the right mix of affordability and academics.

You can use the free service at scholarmatch.org to figure this out. The website gives you a free tool that allows you to input your preferences and lists colleges around the country that match your criteria. You can even screen colleges based on SAT scores needed to apply!

A good tip is to seek the help of your existing instructors and teachers. It is often said that those who truly care, teach. Teachers want their students to excel in life, and if you request their help, they will assist you.

Your English teacher could help you take your application essay up a notch. If you're in college, you can visit the student wellness center and speak to someone who can advise you regarding your personal finances and credit card applications.

These people tend to be business school instructors, so they can provide you with a lot more information than just your personal finances!

All in all, it might seem tough, but being thrifty can take you a long way. Just look at Lil' Dicky. He managed to create an entire music video for his track, $ave Dat Money, without spending a single cent!

If that is the result of spending no money at all, then imagine what you can pull off.

6

EVERYDAY I'M HUSTLIN'

While saving money is great, what really moves the needle is making money. It's easy to get caught up with the idea of reducing expenses at every turn, but the fact is that focusing exclusively on saving money won't be enough.

Perhaps this is why discipline and budgeting has negative connotations in many people's minds. They don't focus enough on the fact that they need to make money as well. The truth is that you don't need to wait until you graduate to start earning money. These days it's easy to earn money while in school.

I started selling candy in school by buying big packages from Costco. I'd noticed kids returning from break with candy from the vending machines and figured there was a way for me to make money. When other kids began offering me money for candy, I became the 'candy kid' and earned $300 for myself.

Admittedly, this was a risky (and illegal) thing to do since I wasn't allowed to sell candy in school and I stopped doing this shortly thereafter.

$300 might not sound like a lot but for a kid in school without any expenses, that is a ton of money! In this chapter I'm going to be giving you many examples and methods which you can use to make money.

Please note: I'm not a lawyer or a financial advisor and this is not legal or financial advice.

A good place to begin, when trying to figure out how to make money, is to take a look at those that already are doing it. Did you know that the average millionaire has seven streams of income (Wang, 2020)? What's more, a lot of these streams are passive sources of income.

Passive income is the true generator of wealth. This refers to income that is not connected to your time. For example, if you work a job you get paid an hourly rate. The amount of money you earn is directly tied to the number of hours you spend working.

Your job is thus an active source of income. Passive income on the other hand doesn't have a direct, one-to-one relationship with the amount of time you spend. For example, if you start a YouTube channel that becomes popular, you earn money around the clock. What's more, your older videos keep making money once you've uploaded them.

You will need to spend time maintaining the channel but it's not as if spending five hours will bring you X amount of money. You can create quality content in three hours or three days. The better your content is, the more money you make. The time spent creating it isn't directly tied to the amount of money you'll earn.

While passive income sounds great, it is the active sources of income that provide you with money to invest in passive sources. For example, investing in stocks or in crowdfunded real estate requires money. This money needs to come from somewhere. The only source for this money is your savings.

That's why it's important to save money by reducing your expenses. You can put that money to work and get it to grow on autopilot. If you have a business idea, then you'll probably need capital to make it work. If you don't have capital, you'll need time. For example, if you want to start a new blog but don't have the time to do so, you'll need to hire writers, which will cost you money.

If you don't hire writers, you'll need to spend time on it yourself. Entrepreneurs need to make these choices when starting and running a business. Having an active source of money removes a lot of financial pressure off and gives you the choice of creating a passive business.

There is a misconception that entrepreneurs are people who take huge amounts of risk with their endeavors. It is true that the average entrepreneur assumes higher levels of risk than the average person, but what sets the entrepreneur apart is how they balance risk and reward.

Starting a business is risky and cash isn't guaranteed. However, if you have enough savings to pay for your living expenses, and you save money from having a steady job while starting a business on the side, your risk is covered. This justifies your decision to adopt the risk of starting a business in pursuit of the rewards it brings.

If you quit everything and started the business, that would be a bad choice since you're not leaving yourself anything to fall back on. For example, Mark Zuckerberg started Facebook in college and dropped out in his sophomore year without completing his degree. If Facebook failed, he always had the option of going back to college and completing his degree.

This is how entrepreneurs make decisions. It isn't about taking huge risks. It's about managing them and making sure they're commensurate with the rewards they offer. So, what are some of the best ways to make money when you're a student. Let's begin by looking at side hustle ideas. These are active sources of income that you can implement to make additional cash outside of school hours.

SIDE HUSTLES

A side hustle is something you do outside of your primary work or school hours. Running a side hustle is a great education by itself because it teaches you to manage your time well. You should not sacrifice study time to run your side hustle.

If you find yourself having to do this, you're probably taking on too much at once. See if you can reduce your workload and manage your time better.

Deliver Stuff

Can you become a delivery driver for the local pizza place? This is a great way to monetize your vehicle, which tends to be a money pit. It's also a better alternative than driving for Uber or other ride sharing companies since you won't have to accommodate other people in your vehicle.

Larger companies, such as DoorDash, allow you to start earning immediately and the best part is you can work flexible hours. If your class schedule shifts, you can always opt for other time slots. There are no vehicle inspections or anything of the kind, just sign-up and earn extra income.

The typical income level for delivery drivers is around $500 per month. It could be even more if you earn tips.

Online Surveys

These side hustlers everywhere. The premise is simple. You take surveys that are created by marketers and, upon completion, you receive a reward such as a gift card or cash. Here are some great websites to get started:

- Survey Junkie
- Swagbucks
- MyPoints
- Opinion Outpost
- PineCone
- Branded Surveys

Aside from surveys there are many other ways you can make money on these websites. For example, you can get paid to search the internet using Swagbucks. Some of the tasks on these websites require simple data entry, reading text and so on.

Amazon's Mechanical Turk is a great resource for such task-oriented jobs. You get paid a few cents for a few minutes of work. This adds up over time and you can potentially earn close to $150 doing this kind of work.

Fiverr Gigs

Fiverr.com is a website for freelancers and there is no limit to the kind of gigs that you can find. Some of the more bizarre gigs I've seen are people offering to release live fish back into rivers, read scripts as Yoda, or provide tinder openers, for example.

While the base price for all gigs is $5, you can charge as much as you want by offering additional services. The price you charge depends on how much demand there is for your service. Either way, this is a great way to earn money on the side and use a skill you have. I know I've mentioned a bizarre list of ideas, but I'm sure you can think of more useful skills to help others and make a few extra bucks!

Selling on eBay and Etsy

Selling your stuff on eBay has been a popular method of making additional cash for a while now. Ever since the website started, people have carried out what's called eBay arbitrage. This means you look for items that are selling for a lot on eBay and then source them cheaply from estate sales or vintage shops.

While the earning potential of this has been declining of late, you can always sell the stuff you don't need on eBay for additional cash. This includes stationery, your textbooks and just about anything else you can think of.

If you're artistic and can create stuff with your hands, then Etsy is a great way to make money from your art. You can sell all kinds of creations on Etsy to make a few extra dollars. Sourcing these items cheaply, or creating them yourself, can result in a potential windfall for you.

Tutoring

Know someone who is struggling with their grades? Offer to tutor them! Many colleges have tutoring departments and you can apply for one of these jobs. Additionally, if you're in college, you can tutor high school students online, for help with their SATs or other tests.

If you happen to be an expert at something, a great place where you can share your experience and get paid for it is clarity.fm. This website allows people to search for those who have expertise in certain areas and seek answers.

While there are the usual experts in entrepreneurship and so on, there are also opportunities to consult in a variety of other subjects. Much like Fiverr, there are many sub niches for you to explore.

Writing and Proofreading

If you're a great writer, there are a number of opportunities available to you. With many businesses going online, there is a high demand for writers and editors. This comes under the bracket of SEO writing and it is a skill that pays well once you've established credibility.

Proofreading is another skill that's in high demand. Bloggers need people who can proofread their posts and give them tips on how to improve their content. A good proofreader or editor can earn as much as $500 per month on the side.

Lastly, the rise of YouTube means that transcribing services are in demand. YouTubers need people who can transcribe their videos to make it easier to create blog posts. It also helps with YouTube SEO. Aside from YouTube, transcription has been a skill that continues to grow in demand.

There are websites, such as TranscribeMe, that offer training and opportunities for transcription, even if you are a complete newbie. Beginner level transcribers can earn around $10 per hour of transcribed audio, while more experienced transcriptionists can earn $30+ per transcribed hour.

e-book Publishing

If you're a great writer and think you have a good story to tell, writing and publishing your e-book on Amazon is a great way to make money. While publishing on Amazon is competitive, writing books that are in demand and assembling a list of reviewers is a great way to earn passive income.

Once you've written and published your book, you'll continue to earn royalties on those sales forever. As you increase the number of books you've published, your royalties increase. While exact numbers are hard to find, you can potentially earn $100 per book, per month, by publishing on Amazon. Best of all, you can sell your book as an e-book, paperback and audio-book and earn royalties from three different streams.

Selling Photos

Are you an avid photographer? If so, you can make money by listing your photos on websites such as Shutterstock, which will pay you every time someone buys your photo. While the royalties per photo are low, it doesn't cost you anything to click additional photos.

You can build a library of photos on these websites that contain hundreds of thousands of photos. All those cents you earn on your photos will begin adding up over time. Like with book royalties, this income is completely passive once you've done the initial work.

User Testing

Websites are springing up every day and there is increased emphasis on user experience. This means there is a demand for having websites tested. Services provided by companies such as Userfeel and Usertesting allow businesses to have their websites tested.

You can sign up to be a website tester and all it takes is a working microphone. It doesn't have to be a great one either. The website will ask you to download a screen capture software and you'll need to talk aloud as you perform tasks.

The earning potential from this can be significant. Depending on the number of tests available, you can earn around $500 per month. You can conduct tests on your laptop as well as on your phone.

Virtual Assistant

People are busy and as their business grows, they need assistance with running them. Larger websites have social media accounts with tons of website related tasks that need to be carried out every day. This is where virtual assistants come into the picture. VAs, as they're called, perform a range of tasks, from setting personal calendars to moderating comments on blogs to monitoring social media.

This will give you great experience in terms of learning how an online business works if you're looking at starting something of your own. The best place to sign up and find VA work is either Fiverr or Upwork.

Cold emailing blog owners is one way to inquire about potential work. You can earn a steady $300 or more per month; highly skilled VAs can earn $3000+ per month.

Teach English

This is one of the most popular ways of making money and also traveling for free. There are many websites that offer English teaching services. While the higher end websites, catering to schools, require you to have TESOL certification, you don't need this if you're marketing yourself or teaching adult learners.

It is good to have these certifications, but websites such as iTalki or Verbalplanet don't require applicants to possess them. Create a website for yourself and a LinkedIn profile and you'll find that people will search for you and inquire about your services.

Dog Walking

If you love animals this could be your dream job! If you happen to live near a suburban area where people tend to have a lot of pets, you could approach them and offer to take their dogs out for a walk. People have busy schedules and this will be a great way for you to get paid while having fun and exercising at the same time!

You can advertise by posting flyers and using direct mail postcards. Putting the word out through your parents and their friends also leads to opportunities. If you have more time on your hands, you could always offer to pet sit for longer periods of time and make even more cash.

House Sitting and Pet Sitting

This is a side hustle where payment varies depending on what your aim is. The premise is simple. If someone goes on vacation but is worried about leaving their homes empty or their pets by themselves, you can offer to look after the place. Breaking into this requires a bit of luck but if you can pull it off, it's a great gig.

Ideally, you'll know someone, either through your network or your parents', who will give you an opportunity to look after their house for them. Once this is done, create a profile on a house sitting site such as Trusted House Sitters or Nomador, and have them leave you a review.

Then, you can apply for other house sits. The key is to have reviews as trust is a major issue with this line of work. The same applies for pet sits. It's best if you can include pictures of you around animals on your personal social media accounts. People will want to check how familiar you are with animals and whether you know what you're doing.

As for compensation, local house sits typically will offer some compensation. However, the real charm of house and pet sitting is that you can travel to another place and live for free. Some owners will compensate for your food and flight expenses as well, so it's a great way to get paid to travel.

Mystery Shopping

Do you love shopping? How would you like to get paid to do it? Think of this as being an offline version of website testing. You can apply to be a mystery shopper on websites such as Field Agent or Secret Shopper and you'll be given assignments to shop at certain stores and report back on your experience.

This isn't an open-ended experience by the way. You will have to follow a strict protocol when shopping and will need to answer specific questions that the client needs answering. But you can earn $100 per month and above with this. Many of the secret shops are for restaurants, so you usually get a free meal as well.

Odd Jobs

If you have a head for maintenance, pool cleaning, lawn mowing or even shoveling snow, these can be great ways to earn additional money. Handyman services are always appreciated and, depending on the skill you have, you could earn a lot of cash from them.

Providing such services can also be a good way to learn about real estate maintenance if you plan on owning property some day. You can also translate these services into a part-time job with a building contractor which will allow you to learn more about the business.

Part-time contracting job rates vary but you can expect to earn around $15 per hour as a trainee. Keep in mind that you won't be earning this much immediately. You will need to build your skills up first.

Plasma Donation

This is a steady favorite on many campuses. Donating blood plasma can bring in anywhere from $20 to $40 per donation. Prior to donating you will be tested for a variety of factors surrounding drug use and other risks to your health. Donating plasma isn't a steady source of income but it can provide you with emergency cash should you need some.

Modeling

If you look good in front of a camera and love posing for

photos, this could be a great side hustle. The best place to find modeling gigs is on Craigslist. Keep your safety in mind and don't accept jobs that expect you to be paid 'in exposure.'

This is when a photographer won't pay you cash and will expect you to derive compensation from the fact that your face appeared in a magazine somewhere. This is a common practice many low-level photographers engage in. But, if you're truly interested in a modeling career, it might be something to consider.

If you're looking for a side hustle, accepting anything other than cash is a non-starter.

Loan Signing Agent and Notary

This is a lesser known side hustle that can make you a ton of money. Loan documents need to be signed in the presence of a person called a signing agent. As official as that sounds, all you need to do is show up with the paperwork given to you and point to the places the signee needs to sign.

The catch is that you need to be trained. Loan Signing System is the highest rated course online and it will show you how you can get jobs in the industry. Once you're trained, you can approach local realtors to inquire about opportunities.

Loan signing agents can make between $75 to $200 per hour depending on experience.

. . .

TaskRabbit

TaskRabbit is a website where people post a number of small tasks that need to be done and you can get paid money to complete these tasks. The most popular tasks involve delivering things, lifting heavy stuff, assembling furniture and cleaning.

Perform enough tasks and you can earn around $300 per month from them.

As you can see, there are tons of ways for you to make money when you're a student. This is over and above any jobs you can find on or off campus. If you're studying for a technical degree, then applying for a paid internship or a co-op with a company in your field will have huge benefits for your career.

All of these options involve you spending time and getting compensated for it. To really double your earning potential, you need to build passive sources of income. Let's take a look now at the ways in which you can make money passively.

PASSIVE INCOME SOURCES

The options you're going to learn about are a mixture of starting businesses and purely passive sources of income. Which ones you choose depends on your psyche and what appeals to you. Generally speaking, it's a good idea to start building sources of passive income as soon as possible.

This is because passive income sources often start paying rewards down the road and not immediately. You will need patience but it isn't uncommon for the methods mentioned below to begin earning you close to $1,000 per month a year after you begin.

Some of these methods will require time investment upfront since you need to spend time creating them. Think of them as being assets that will pay you money down the road, much like a piece of property would. The best part is that your expense on these assets is minimal and you can even launch a career through them.

Stock Investing

The stock market can both make you money over the long-term and provide you with cash over the short-term. There are two ways to make money in stocks. The first is called capital gains. If you buy a stock for $5 and sell it for $10, you've earned a $5 profit. This is a capital gain.

The second way is through dividends. Dividends are cash payouts some stocks make to their investors. Typically, you can expect to receive around one to two percent of your investment as a dividend on a dividend paying stock. So, if you buy stock worth $100 you can expect a dividend of $1 or $2.

This isn't much to start, but if you keep reinvesting your money into the stock, your payouts will increase. Keep in mind that not all stocks pay dividends. Investing in the stock market as early as possible is a good idea and you should start building your portfolio. Instead of investing in individual companies, put your money in index funds that track the entire market.

This reduces your risk and will guarantee that you will receive market average gains. Sign up for a brokerage account with Robinhood and you can invest for free in stocks. Apps such as Acorns allows you to budget as well as invest.

Acorns, in particular, rounds off your expenses to the nearest dollar and invests that into a fund that tracks the entire stock market. This way, your investing is automated. While you won't earn huge levels of cash flow from stock market investing (unless your investment is huge), it pays off over a long period of time.

P2P Lending

P2P stands for peer to peer. Here's how it works. You sign up for an account at a website such as Prosper. This allows you to view loan requests from many people. You will see the loan amount requested, their credit rating and the interest you will earn by lending them money.

These platforms will even allow you to invest your money in pre-designed portfolios so you don't need to assess individual borrowers one by one. It's a great way to automate your cash flow. There are no minimum investment requirements. You can invest $100 into a portfolio and it gets divided across the borrowers in that portfolio.

You can expect to earn five to six percent returns on your investment. So, if you invest $100, you can expect a return of $5 or $6. Again, this doesn't sound like much but remember that this is free money. You're not working for it.

Savings Accounts and CDs

CD stands for certificate of deposit. When you put a certain amount of money into it, you'll earn an interest rate for a period of time. During this time, you will not be allowed to withdraw those funds. Savings accounts, as the name suggests, pay you an interest rate on the funds held in the account.

Typically, savings accounts will pay you 0.5% interest on your account balance. This is pretty abysmal, so if you have some cash to spare and don't need it for a year or so, a CD is a good option. CDs with online banks can return 1.8% on your deposit.

Create a Blog or Social Media Channel

This comes firmly under the online business category. There are tons of ways to monetize a blog. Here are some of them;

- Affiliate marketing - send your readers/viewers to a link and earn a commission if they buy the product or service.
- Sell your own product - Create a course or write a book.
- Sell services - Sell consulting services

- Advertising - Enable ads on your website and sign up for ad networks.
- Partner with brands - Sell brand products on your channels and get compensated to advertise them. Or get free samples. Travel bloggers with large enough audiences, get free vacations.

There are many ways to monetize your blog or social media channel. The best part is that it costs almost nothing to start a blog. You'll need $14 to buy a domain name and will need to pay around $3 per month to host your website. Choose a topic you like and start writing.

Opening a YouTube or social media account is free. If you have knowledge in a particular area or are curious enough to research it thoroughly, create videos on the topic and post them on YouTube. You can monetize your channel by running ads or redirect them to products you're affiliated with.

Instagram is a popular way to earn money. While the influencer space is maligned and is increasingly crowded, the platform remains a great way to monetize your appeal. An influencer who has a million followers can earn anywhere between $2,500 to $4,000 per post.

Think of all of these channels as being assets in your business. Your blog is digital real estate and owning a piece of the internet is extremely valuable. It takes around a year at the very least for some kind of money to start flowing in, but if you develop a plan to create content and perform the right research, you will see your earnings jump.

Once it does this, running the blog or social media channel becomes a matter of maintaining your business. Your earnings also increase exponentially as the slightest effort will pay larger dividends.

The best way to get started is to invest in yourself and learn how to go about building online presence. Follow the right steps and you'll find that this kind of income is really the best!

Print on Demand

If you're the artistic type and love creating designs, then getting into POD or print on-demand services is a great opportunity. Websites such as Amazon (Merch by Amazon) and Teespring allow you to upload your designs for free. They then display those designs on t-shirts, coffee mugs or posters and viewers can order them.

Every time someone orders a product with your design on it, you get paid. Simple! Keep in mind that this is a crowded space so you will need to publicize your designs and drive traffic to them. To do this, it helps to have a popular social media account or a blog.

POD is a great way to sell products that can build your brand and make your business even more popular.

.   .   .

International Markets

Do you speak a second language? Are you extremely fluent in it to the extent that you can create videos and write blogs in it? If so, you could be sitting on a goldmine. Aside from launching a translation business, you should definitely consider exploring niches in those foreign markets.

The reason for this is simple. Traffic in foreign markets is cheap. Let's take POD as an example. What many designers do is they upload their designs and then run Facebook ads to drive traffic to them. These days, this tactic is guaranteed to fail because Facebook traffic is extremely expensive.

Facebook makes money every time someone clicks your ad so it is in their best interest to increase the cost per click. In other words, every time someone clicks your ad, you get charged a high amount. This makes it impossible for you to make a profit after selling your product.

However, in foreign markets, not only is traffic cheap but competition is less expensive, as well. A financial blog in English will stand close to no chance of ranking, thanks to Google prioritizing the authority of the writer. However, there aren't many financial authority blogs in Danish and as a result, whoever creates relevant content will stand a better chance of ranking at the top.

The second language market is extremely lucrative and can be applied to every single money-making idea online. If you published a book in English, get it translated into German, Spanish and French. If your YouTube videos are in English, create subtitles or have a voice-over in another language.

Even better, if you speak the language, create the content yourself. You'll build an audience literally around the world and will unlock new avenues of making money.

Vending Machines and ATMs

Vending machines are a great business but require some hustle to turn in to a success. You will need to invest money in a machine and then scout good locations for it. Once you find one, you will need to develop a good relationship with the landlord and service it regularly.

The best part about the business is that it is completely passive once you've done the initial work. Don't mistake passive for easy. You will face competition and this can be cut-throat. You might find that the landlord cancels your contract and installs their own machine in the location.

Some of your machines might be broken into and the money stolen. These are a part of the business that you'll have to deal with. The ATM business is pretty much the same. You can make the ATM business completely passive by hiring someone to manage it for you.

If you have the capital to invest, these can be good money-making options. Additionally, if you don't mind hustling and staying ahead of the competition, then these businesses will prove to be extremely lucrative for you.

Alexa Skills

Forget about developing an app, start developing Alexa Skills instead. Let's backup a bit since you might not be fully aware of what Alexa is. Alexa is Amazon's voice assistant program, much like Cortana for Microsoft and Siri for Apple. Alexa is currently available in the Echo speaker that Amazon sells.

The Echo can connect to smart devices around your home and allows you to automate a number of tasks. Much like how you can install an app on your phone to carry out certain tasks, you can install a Skill from the Alexa Skills store to enable Alexa to carry out tasks around your home.

These range from reading the news to providing updates on stock prices. You can also install Skills that are word games the entire family can play, for example. The opportunity lies in creating these Skills and publishing them to the Skills store.

Initially, creating a Skill required coding knowledge but these days you can use Amazon's Alexa Skill Blueprints to create a Skill and publish it to the store. All Skills are currently free as mandated by Amazon. However, you have the option of adding in Skill purchases.

In addition to this, Amazon rewards the best performing Skills in certain categories with huge bonuses every month. If you have programming knowledge, you can seek clients and build Skills for them, thereby allowing you to start a development agency.

The Echo is the most popular home automation device at the moment, and it is only growing in usage. The best part of this industry is that once users adopt a particular home assistant, they're unlikely to shift to another. In other words, if you like Alexa, you're not going to be comfortable using Siri or Google Home Assistant in the future.

The competition is still low in this field so if you can come up with a creative idea for a Skill, you stand to earn a lot of money. Developers of popular Skills regularly receive payouts over $5,000 from Amazon.

Invest in a Business

While P2P lending allows you to invest in debt (that is, loan someone money), equity crowdfunding allows you to invest in someone's business in exchange for a cut of the profits from it. I must mention that such investment is extremely risky and you should think twice before investing in such opportunities.

Here's how it works. A business needs cash to finance its operation and it creates a campaign where it solicits funds from people. In exchange for your contribution, you receive shares in the business. Some businesses require a minimum investment of $1,000 and above, but some have lower minimums.

Investing in such businesses is a lot like investing in a company in the stock market. You will need to conduct your research thoroughly. The flip side is that if you do make a good investment, your rewards are substantial. These companies tend to be startups and as they become successful, their growth becomes exponential.

Investing a small amount can result in a huge payout so it might be worth exploring this option.

Create Courses

If you happen to be knowledgeable about a particular topic, create a course around it on Udemy. Udemy is the biggest resource for learning new skills and there is no limit to the number of courses you can create. Currently, you can take a course on Star Trek along with a course on bio-mechanics.

While there are many categories for you to explore here, keep in mind that a course that you create is best paired with a website or social media channel you can use to drive traffic to it.

Play Games

What was your parents' nightmare has turned into a viable option to generate serious cash. Playthroughs of popular games, recordings of play sessions and rivalry sessions, are big business, with many games signing exclusive deals with streaming companies such as YouTube and Twitch.

. . .

The latter is the biggest video game streaming community on the planet and hosts a whole range of players. This really is a wide-open field. There's even a grandma making money by recording her sessions on Skyrim.

Even if you aren't a gamer, there's a lot of potential in creating mixes of popular gaming moments using creative commons videos on YouTube, and uploading them onto your channel. As traffic builds up, you can make money using affiliate links to gaming related websites.

Technically, you can do this with any niche but it's most effective when done with gaming since the players are extremely passionate.

This brings us to the end of our look at the various ways you make money online. As you can see, there are many options out there. All you need is just one of them to work and you'll put yourself in a much better position financially. Once you build a source of income, parlay that into an investment in another and watch your wealth snowball.

It will be slow going at first but, over time, you'll manage to build multiple streams of passive income and will be well on your way to financial independence.

7

SAVE MONEY BY FINDING THE RIGHT CAREER

Our life goals change as we grow older, and often, the things we find interesting change along with it. Taking the time when you're a student to really figure out what you want to do with your life is not only a smart move, it's also the fiscally responsible one.

This is because you don't want to be the student who is halfway through college and then figures out they're studying the wrong thing. Switching courses at this stage will cost you both time and money. It pays to take your interests out for a test drive, so to speak, before committing to them.

Our first passion often comes from our parents. My father wanted to be a doctor but couldn't pursue this, partly because I was born. As I grew up, I always wanted to be a doctor because I thought this would help him fulfill his dream. I volunteered in high school at a hospital and quickly discovered that I was extremely uncomfortable at the sight of blood.

Being a doctor was out for me! My father was disappointed but he understood. I then decided to study business and my father gave me some of the best advice I've ever received. He told me to drop out of school because I didn't need a degree to start a business. However, if my mind was made up, I needed to study a specific business niche, so that my money would be well invested.

I inquired at the school and found myself in a conversation with a professor who mentioned that supply-chain and logistics were booming career fields. He mentioned that the day-to-day tasks involved challenging situations and that every day was a puzzle that needed to be solved.

This sounded fascinating and I've been in this field ever since! While everyone finds their own way forward in life, this doesn't mean there aren't things that you can do to bring yourself closer to your purpose quicker. Asking what you want to do in life is a big question.

Answering this question requires us to explore the concept of Ikigai.

IKIGAI

The concept of Ikigai was first talked about in a book of the same name authored by Albert Liebermann and Hector Garcia (Garcia, Miralles, Cleary & Garcia, 2016). The authors came across the concept when they ran into a startling fact in their research on the Japanese island of Okinawa.

This island has the biggest population of centenarians (people over the age of 100) in the world. In addition to this place, spots such as the Mediterranean island of Sardinia and the Nicoya Peninsula off the coast of Costa Rica had similarly high concentrations of centenarians as well.

Intrigued, they began researching why this was the case and found that the only explanation for such long life spans was the attitude that the people in these parts of the world adopted towards life. While the name Ikigai is Japanese, the principles it espouses are very similar to what is followed in the other parts of the world as well.

It is often represented as four circles intersecting one another. The four circles represent the following:

- What you love
- What you're good at
- What you can get paid for
- What the world needs

In short, a person's Ikigai is at the intersection of what they're good at, what they love doing, what they can get paid for and what the world needs. Finding this is easier said than done! Most of us know what we like to do, but we don't really know how to figure out if we can get paid to do it. What's more, the things we like to do keep changing all the time.

The process of finding your Ikigai helps you move towards your ultimate purpose in life. It is a philosophy as opposed to an object or a phenomenon. The foundational tenets of Ikigai state that finding your purpose is a journey and it isn't about reaching a goal.

For example, you might find that you love drawing and you begin sketching. This might lead you to exploring graphic design as a career. Once you're in graphic design, you might find that you're interested in the elements that go into creating a successful sales page. This leads you into the world of User Experience design or UX.

UX in turn can lead you to explore other elements of successful digital marketing and you could end up creating a course about this and establishing your own consulting practice. Your love for drawing led you to running your own business. Who says all artists starve?

The point of this story is that our purpose is a path and not a goal. This is what Ikigai states. Therefore, every step of the way, you might find that the things you like and the things you consider important will change. This doesn't mean you're being indecisive.

It simply means you've progressed further along the path to finding your purpose.

The Process

Despite being a philosophy, the framework of Ikigai provides a very clear set of steps to conduct in order to find your purpose. Before you begin, make sure you can set aside 30 minutes to finish these steps. You can do this with friends or by yourself. Remember to not discuss what you write among yourselves until the end.

The first step is to take a notebook and draw a line horizontally, and a line vertically, through the middle of a page; you should have four square areas on your page. Next, label the four areas, or quadrants with the names of the corresponding Ikigai circles. Start from the top left quadrant and move in a counter clock-wise direction.

Label them in order as 'what you love' (top left), 'what are you good at' (top right), 'what can you get paid for' (this will be the bottom right corner) and 'what the world needs (bottom left).' The third step for you to take is to start filling the sections in turn. The idea is to allow your brain to simply throw everything it can think of, and for you to record it without judgment or hesitation.

Don't involve your brain too much or rationalize your thoughts. Take around three to five minutes to complete each section.

What You Love

This should be an easy section to fill! Don't worry about making money from these things or anything rational like that. A good way to think about filling this section is to ask yourself what are the things you've never gotten bored with? What is something that keeps pulling you back in?

Is there something you do that causes you to lose track of time, to the extent that you forget to eat and drink? What brings about this type of a 'flow' state within you?

Remember to list everything that comes into your mind immediately, and don't censor yourself!

What You're Good At

This section encourages you to focus on reality a bit more, and asks what are the things you're good at; either right now, or the things you're learning to become good at. Are there certain skills you've been practicing regularly? Is there some skill you want to be good at? Another clue to figure this out is to ask yourself what do people come to you for help with?

If you can't find specific words to describe these qualities, don't sweat it. Just write them out as phrases. Remember to be as nonjudgmental as possible. Typically, the first thing that pops into your head is the right answer. Drawing might suggest itself but then your brain might peg you back a notch and tell you that you haven't drawn anything for years.

Stick to the original thought and write whatever comes into your mind.

What Can you Get Paid For?

This moves you even more firmly into the practical world. A common mistake people make at this point is to start assimilating the previous two sections and craft appropriate answers here. However, this is not the point. It might help, in fact, to take a day or two between the first two sections, and these final sections. That way your brain can really take a break from thinking too hard about this.

You should ignore the previous sections right now and simply think about what you would like to get paid for. If you're not happy with your current situation, what would you rather study or work at? If you've been paid money to do something before, what was it?

Students may find this particular section tough because you've likely never worked a full-time job before. It doesn't matter if your work history is short or if you've only ever been paid to lift boxes in a warehouse up to this point. Record it and focus on what you would like to get paid to do.

If you want to get paid to observe and study sharks in Fiji, then list this out! This is all about you after all, so don't judge yourself.

What the World Needs

This is another section where most people end up making a mistake. When someone asks you what the world needs, you might think that world peace would be a good start! This question isn't so much about the entire world as much as it is about your world. Think of those around you and in your life.

What could you use more of in your world? More happiness, joy, money etc.? How about a sense of fulfillment? Now, think of those close to you. How could you affect them positively? What could you bring to their world and what kinds of feelings do you want to create in their lives?

If there is someone close to you who needs help of some kind, what do they need in their lives?

Once you've filled out all four sections, take some time to look at everything you've written and add anything else you think is appropriate. Once done, move onto the next step.

Finding Your Ikigai

Now comes the most exciting step! Look through the four sections and find the thing that is in common. It could be a theme or an activity or a particular action that stands out. Once you've found this commonality, that's your Ikigai!

You might discover that the four sections have nothing in common and this is okay. Remember that finding your Ikigai is about making the journey and isn't about reaching a destination. Take your time with the process, even if it takes you months, or years to complete.

Keep revisiting the four sections. Add new material to them and ask yourself tough questions. This is all about you, so don't write down answers that you think the world or someone close to you might find appropriate. It's your life and you get to decide how you want to live it.

Finding your calling in life takes a while and you'll find that your interests will change with time. This is perfectly fine. Be patient and keep following the process. You'll certainly find the thing that you love the most!

CHOOSING THE RIGHT CAREER

Choosing the right job and career path is one of the most important decisions you will make in your life. The fact is that research shows over 70% of workers are unhappy with their careers (O'Donnell, 2020). Why is this? How is it possible that so many people end up choosing the wrong jobs?

The problem lies within us. From a young age we are conditioned to chase rewards for the tasks that we complete. If you study hard, you get good grades. If you work a lot of hours, you get paid and so on. This directly impacts the validation centers within our brain, as you learned when you read about the impact social media has on your brain.

Wanting to be admired and liked activates our pleasure centers quite strongly, and this often results in us choosing to work in jobs that we think other people will approve of. This is why I stressed in the previous section that you should not write answers that you think other people will like.

Choosing a career on the basis of external motivation like this will lead you to becoming one of the 70% that dislike their jobs. Consider that you'll spend the majority of your days as a professional at work. That's over a third of your life spent working. If you feel miserable all the time, you're probably not doing what you love and your earning potential will decrease.

The qualitative effects of work dissatisfaction are even worse. You're likely to have bad relationships with your family and are at a high risk of becoming depressed or anxious (O'Donnell, 2020). So, how likely is it that you'll pick a career for external rather than internal reasons?

A good place to start is to ask yourself: Do you judge other people on the basis of what they do? It's important to be honest with your answer. When you meet someone new is 'what do you do' one of the first questions you ask them? Do you judge their answer as either 'good' or 'bad?'

Many people indulge in this kind of behavior and that's okay. The minute someone introduces themselves as a doctor, their attitude towards that person changes. If you're someone who does this, odds are good that you will end up picking a career to please other people.

The reason is pretty straightforward. Since you value what other people do and judge them on that basis, you'll want to be judged well yourself. Hence, you're going to pick a nice sounding career that others will approve of, even if it's the worst choice possible for you.

If you're thinking about, or struggling to pick a career, ask the people who work in those fields what they think about their jobs. Most importantly, ask them why they love it. If they truly love it, they'll speak about the connection they feel with their work and the satisfaction it brings.

They'll be willing to put up with the less savory aspects of the job because they get to do what they love. Ask them what their least favorite parts of the job are and see if you'd be willing to put up with all of them. There is no profession that has only good parts after all. You're going to have to deal with the entire package if you want to be successful.

In addition to asking questions, there are three tactics you can use to evaluate what your chosen career path actually looks like.

Shadowing

What better way is there of finding what the job is like than by observing what goes on at work and what the person does all day? This practice is referred to as shadowing and it is something that high school students and early year college students can make use of. There are a wide range of professions that allow students to shadow the professionals who work in them.

Keep in mind that your school's location and proximity to certain industries will dictate available opportunities. For example, a school in New York City is going to have more financial industry shadowing opportunities than one in Carbondale, Illinois. Many schools are affiliated with shadowing programs.

Check with the counselors in your high school or with the career services office in your college to find possible matches. Typically, shadowing programs have certain requirements and procedures you'll need to follow in order to apply and complete the program.

Some will need you to describe why you're looking for a particular shadowing opportunity and to introduce yourself to your mentor before receiving an affirmative answer. Describe what interests you about that field and why you're looking for an opportunity in it.

Also mention what you're looking to learn from the experience. You might have to clear your schedule since the professional's calendar might be packed. You might not always have the chance to shadow a person in your desired profession due to confidentiality reasons. In that case, try to find a profession that is closely related to it.

Another good way to unearth shadowing opportunities is to ask your parents or someone in their network for such opportunities. Checking with any organizations you're a part of or any professional societies on campus is also a good step to take.

Checking shadowing opportunities should be something you must do before picking a major. After all, it doesn't make sense to study something you won't have any interest in doing later on in life. You might have to contact people and ask them for shadowing opportunities. If you get turned down, be polite and thank them for their time.

If you receive an affirmative answer then show up at the right time and dress professionally. It's best to dress in business casual attire unless the dress code of that profession is different. Keep your eyes and ears open throughout the day and switch your phone off.

Take notes on paper as you shadow your mentor and jot down any questions that occur to you. Ask them for answers when you get the appropriate chances. Always conduct some research on the company before you show up. Take note of what is being said about the company in the media or of any particular challenges they're facing.

Are there any new products the company has launched recently? See how the workplace is and how people interact with one another. Working professionals are typically quite enthusiastic about showing students what they do for a living;

as long as you keep out of the way, you'll be welcomed and will probably learn a lot.

You will find that some parts of the day will be boring and that you might not be invited to certain events due to privacy concerns. Remember that your mentor is still working throughout the day and will have to ignore you for certain periods of time in order to do their job. Don't take this person-ally and treat everyone with courtesy.

The more you prepare, the more you'll get out of the experi-ence. At the end of the day, conduct a debrief with your mentor. If you find that you don't want to pursue that job, then that's perfectly fine. You've just learned something and it cost you just one day instead of decades of your life!

Once the experience is finished, remember to send them a thank you note. If you interacted with anyone else who showed you a few pointers, get their business card and send them a quick message as well. Doing this is recommended regardless of whether you intend to pursue that career or not.

Informational Interviews

When shadowing opportunities are not available to you, the informational interview might be the answer!

This is a tactic that is often used by job seekers but it is some-thing that you can also use to your advantage. In many cases, if you happen to like the job, it can even help you get your foot in the door. Informational interviews can be set up with people as a second option if they decline your shadowing request.

A great way to find people to interview is to hop onto LinkedIn and create a profile. As a student, you're not going to attract many offers but you can connect with people on the platform. If you can afford it, opt for the premium membership which will let you message anyone on the platform, irrespective of whether they're in your network or not.

Send them a thoughtfully crafted email and emphasize what you want to learn. This is pretty much the same as what you'll do when asking someone for a shadowing request. Mention that you'll need an hour of their time and that your schedule is open.

You'll probably get 30 minutes to an hour at the most, so you'll need to prepare your questions well. Generally speaking, your objective is to figure out what the professional likes about their job and what they dislike about it. If you feel that you can put up with the negatives, then choosing that profession might be the smart thing to do.

Even though you're the one interviewing them, it helps to approach the interview as if you're the one being interviewed. Dress appropriately and conduct thorough research on the company before going to your meeting. Make sure that when you meet them to ask them how their day is going, and establish a nice rapport.

As you dive into specific questions that you might have about their job, make sure to ask them what kind of mentorship they receive in their career. This is an important question to ask, since a career that has growth opportunities will leave you feeling more fulfilled than one that has a low ceiling. You'll also want to ask about the money they earn but you need to go about it subtly. Check online what the salary ranges are and ask them if these ranges are accurate.

If the ranges are too wide, then you can narrow them down to get a more accurate figure. For example, if the range you see online is $65,000 to $90,000 per year, ask them if a range of $80-90,000 is accurate. They'll correct you or confirm the range and you'll have a better idea of how much money you may make.

Once the interview is finished, thank them for their time and make sure you get their business card. Send them a thank you note, no matter what your decision ultimately is.

Internships

If shadowing and informational interviews don't work out for you, you can opt for internships. If you do decide to pursue a career in a certain field, applying for a paid (or unpaid) internship is the best way to build relationships within a company; it is also a great way to graduate with a job offer.

If you want to explore what a career is all about, and if paid internships aren't available, work for free! This might sound like an odd thing to do but interns who work for free typically receive a lot of input in what the field is like. Companies genuinely appreciate such workers and teach them everything they know.

It might be challenging remaining motivated on an unpaid internship but look at this as an extension of your school tuition. No one pays you to go to school either and, in fact, you pay huge sums of money to attend. With an unpaid internship, you get to learn everything for free!

WHAT KIND OF DEGREE?

Many students commonly think that a four or five year bachelor's degree is the best option, but this is not always the case. Many professions require nothing more than an associate's degree and you can begin working in as little as two years.

What's more, the credits you earn from an associate's degree can be transferred to a bachelor's degree. For example, you could earn an associate of science in mechanical engineering technology and score a job as a mechanical engineering technician.

The average salary of this job is $55,360 and your credits will transfer towards a full-fledged bachelor's degree. A bachelor's degree will earn you a salary of $70,500 on average and it has more career growth potential. However, you can earn an associate's in two years and fund the bachelor's degree with the money you save from it. In short, you get the best of all worlds!

Those interested in the legal profession will also find that you can become a paralegal with just an associate's degree. This will help you build a network within law firms. You'll find that many firms have programs that fund the education of their associates, provided they're willing to work with the firm for a few years after graduation.

A job that is slightly out of left field, but is extremely lucrative, is that of an air traffic controller. Keep in mind that this is a highly stressful job but it only requires a two-year associate of science degree in aeronautics. The average salary of a controller is $124,000.

Programming and software development are two industries that typically need just two-year associate's degrees. In these cases, pursuing a full-fledged bachelor's degree might not make the most sense. In addition to this, certificates in these fields matter a lot more than degrees. So, if you're interested in technology and programming, then getting an associate's degree and then working on various certifications may be the best path forward.

So, conduct your research thoroughly before deciding on what kind of education you want. Speak to professionals and use the three methods you've just learned about to figure out what the job is like. You'll find that, with the right degree, you'll make money sooner and will be in a better position to fund further education.

Options for High School Students

There is one particular option that high school students can opt for and this is to choose a dual enrollment program. Under the terms of these programs, students can complete two years' worth of college-level courses in high school, for no additional charge in most states. Even if you do have to pay, there are tuition assistance programs available.

This is a bit like taking your college major out for a test drive. You will receive a taste of college-level course loads and you can figure out whether your chosen major is the right one for you. If you do like your courses, you can graduate with a bachelor's degree in two years and save big on college tuition.

Many high schools do a less than perfect job of promoting these programs and you should take the time to inquire about them. There are many positives to these programs. These include:

- The college-level classes you take, along with the relevant textbooks, are free and will be paid for by your high school. All you'll have to do is fill out a form.
- Unlike AP classes, where you earn credit only when you pass the final exam (irrespective of whether you pass the class), dual enrollment programs allow you to

earn credit solely upon passing the class. This means you don't need to pay for taking that class again in college; this reduces the time you need to earn your degree in college.

- By taking college-level courses, you're not going to be intimidated about the level of work you'll have to get used to. From personal experience, college simply felt like high school, part two, for me!

- By beginning the program during your sophomore year in high school, you can graduate with both your high school diploma as well as your AA degree. If your school has no cap on how many classes you can take per semester, you can do what I did and take two additional classes per semester. This saved me around $1,800 in college-level tuition!

- Every student who decides to enroll in these programs needs to pass a preliminary test. The subjects are usually Math, Reading and Writing. The best part about this is you will be given all the material you need to pass the exam. As long as you ask for help and study, you'll find that passing this exam is pretty straightforward!

- The credits you earn in the dual enrollment program will count towards your high school GPA as well. For instance, if you need to take English II, you can add the course in your schedule and earn credit for it simultaneously for both college and high school. Talk about killing two birds with one stone!

There are a few disadvantages that you should be aware of as well.

- If your high school has a limit on the number of classes you can take per semester, this is going to hurt your chances of significantly reducing the cost of tuition you'll need to pay in college.
- Since the classes will be held away from your high school, you will need to find transportation in order to attend classes, unless online versions are available.
- You might find your day stretching on too long, since you'll have to take these classes right after school. You can schedule them for the times that suit you but there are typically no weekend class options.
- Lastly, if you take classes in summer, you'll not have much of a social life, even if you are saving loads of money!

These programs offer huge advantages overall and the pros far outweigh the cons, in my opinion. Perhaps the biggest benefit is that you can begin earning money a whole lot quicker!

8

SMART SPENDING FOR
RELATIONSHIPS AND DATING

W hat is the primary cause of marital strife? It's money (Morse, 2020)! Differences in spending and saving patterns, and a lack of communication around spending, are what cause arguments that ultimately end in divorces. Spending money wisely when dating is a tough thing to manage.

A lot of people tend to adopt pets due to the loneliness of being single and this can potentially be a bad financial choice for you. The fact is that our romantic relationships are so fraught with emotion that it's hard to inject practical matters like money into it. For example, you want to impress your date but how can you do this with little money and not come across as a cheapskate?

THE PET QUESTION

Having a pet is great since it provides companionship and leads to greater feelings of fulfillment. You'll be responsible for another being and this has been proved to offer many health benefits (Davis, 2020).

Some people tend to keep a pet to avoid feelings of loneliness, but they often neglect to take the financial considerations of this decision into account. You want to give your pet a good standard of living, so you need to be doubly sure that you can actually afford to keep one for yourself.

A dog is going to cost you a lot more than a goldfish. A cat will cost you something in between. Different animals require varying levels of attention as well, so you need to take your time spent taking care of them into account. You also need to consider the space you can afford to provide your pet with.

Most student housing properties are not suited for dogs. Typically, even small dogs need space. If you're living with many roommates, a bird might drive everyone else crazy, so you'll need to take various factors into account.

Dogs and cats are the most common pets that people adopt and the American Pet Product Association estimates the annual costs of taking care of them as follows ("Pet Industry Market Size & Ownership Statistics," 2020):

1. Boarding - $200
2. Surgical vet visits - $300
3. Routine visits - $180
4. Food - $250
5. Treats - $65
6. Grooming - $50
7. Supplements - $55
8. Toys - $40

These are average annual numbers with the costs for dogs being higher than that for cats. The best way of saving money on these expenses is to shop online. Physical stores charge a huge markup when it comes to pet supplies. Shopping online for medication is also a much better option than purchasing them from a vet.

Another tip is to buy toys that last. These toys will be more expensive than most, but they'll make up for it with their shelf life. If you have a particularly chewy dog, then buying a more expensive chew toy that lasts is a good investment.

DATING ON A BUDGET

Many people believe that you need to spend a ton of money on a date in order to have a great time. But your budget as a student might not extend to paying for a helicopter ride for two around your city, like we see in the movies or on popular "dating" programs! However, this shouldn't stop you from dating!

The purpose of dating is to meet enough people to finally find someone you love and are compatible with. There are two ways you can meet people. The first is to meet them in person and start a conversation with the hope of it leading to a date. The second, and more mainstream method, is to meet someone online.

Dating is meant to be fun but you should keep your safety in mind. Meet them somewhere public when you meet them for the first time. There are tons of ways you can date on the cheap. Here are a few ideas to get you started.

Try a Quiz Night

For those of you over 21, you can have a fun, inexpensive date at the local bar. For example, it's inexpensive and fun to play a game of pool. Some bars have trivia nights or quiz games. Many times, drink specials make the night less expensive, just don't go overboard with your drinking.

Picnics and Movie Dates

These make for great dates, especially in the summer or spring. All you'll need is some sandwich making skills, a thermos of something cool to drink, a basket and a large enough blanket for the two of you. The local park also offers great opportunities to observe things around you, including (sometimes) interesting sights and features. For example, at a park off of Lake Michigan, north of Chicago, there are adult-size swing sets that are very popular with locals and visitors, alike.

You can try a picnic at the local beach as well. You can make the event more fun by deciding to bring half the supplies for the picnic and having your date bring the other half.

The typical dinner and a movie can get expensive really fast and it can be a bit awkward as a first date if there isn't a good connection. Some communities host open-air movie nights, or free plays and concerts in the park. This is a great opportunity for you to pack your own snacks and have an impromptu picnic for dinner!

Romantic Walks

Walks provide you ample opportunity to talk to the other person and to also see if you're compatible with each other. Best of all, a walking date doesn't place any pressure on either of you. You can stroll down and watch the sunset, take a walk in the park or explore a historic neighborhood. Wherever you decide to walk, remember that the point is to have fun! If things aren't working out, you can always cut it short without any repercussions.

Get Touristy

No, I'm not talking about booking a plane ticket to the Caribbean! Many people have no idea what's offered to tourists in the place they live in. After all, we tend to take our own cities for granted. Search for free local attractions or for places that offer discounts to locals. You'll find that a lot of tourist attractions offer 50% or more off to locals; this is a great way to discover your city all over again!

Major metropolitan areas have their share of quirky museums to visit. What's more, these places often offer large student discounts and sometimes hold events that admit people for free. Check online or call these places to figure out what's going on.

For example, New York City has a modern cultural museum that is called Mmuseumm. Here patrons can view cultural oddities such as mosquitoes preserved mid-bite, a vegan shawarma and so on. Best of all, it costs just five dollars (which is the suggested donation amount). Check your local area for weird or quirky museums (or even regular ones).

At Home Date

Instead of heading out, why not stay in and cook something nice together? This is a chance to show off your cooking skills. It can be paired with some great games such as cards, board games or video games. You can even decide to cook a meal together and see how well you work as a team!

Open Mic Nights and Free Events

The quality of talent on show at these fun events is going to be hit or miss but, either way, you'll have something to talk about. There are numerous open mic nights that are organized in every area and college campuses happen to be a hotbed for this kind of event. Take advantage of this and score some free entertainment.

Street food fairs, free concerts, farmers markets, exhibitions and so on are great events to visit with your date. Search for events in your area online or on ticket booking websites. You might find some really weird and fun things to do that will certainly provoke conversation.

You can check your school's website for listings or use apps such as Everbites or Meetup to find events in your area.

Sport and Action

If both of you love being active, then going for a run or getting a workout in together is a great way to bond. You could go on a cycling tour or go hiking. Even better, you could teach one another some of your hobbies.

Pick Fruit and Vegetables

If you happen to live in a rural area, check to see if any fruit and vegetable picking farms are around you. These make for great dates and you can pick fresh fruit or veggies! This is a pretty healthy option for a date. You can even pair this with a picnic or a home cooked meal afterwards. This might not be an option for all seasons, since it might rain and you might not be in the right season for it.

· · ·

Go Bowling

Bowling alleys offer great deals during off-peak hours and give you ample opportunity to connect with your date. They're also great places for double-dates in case you're nervous. Bowling alleys also offer snacks and additional attractions that will prevent your date from going stale.

Search for coupons and offers and remember to have a good time! Also remember to carry your student ID in case there are discounts offered.

The Errand Date

This sounds a little boring but hear me out. Errands are pretty boring and monotonous to carry out, so why not add a bit of fun to them? Let's say you need to buy a paper shredder but everything you see online costs $50 or more.

Why not check out a flea market to see if you can find a cheaper one instead? You can walk around looking at stuff that's weird and try to find the most ridiculous item on sale. Pair this with a walk around the park or neighborhood and you have the recipe for a perfect evening.

Chances are you'll have such a great time that your date will volunteer for the next errand!

Use Coupons

You don't need to carry around a bunch of clipped coupons in your wallet. Instead, shop around for offers that restaurants are running. You can also use Groupon to avoid the hassle of carrying paper coupons. Many places offer deals that are great for dates, such as two for one deals or 50% discounts.

You can even boast to your date about a great deal that you found to dine at a fancy Japanese steakhouse or for a kayaking trip. The quality of the experience will lead to a great date and it will be that much sweeter since you managed to save money doing it!

TALKING ABOUT MONEY

When your relationship moves into a phase where you've been dating for a while and you are getting more serious (maybe even discussing marriage), you'll need to start talking to one another about your finances. This brings its own problems. Let's face it. It's awkward to talk about money, especially with your partner. Money and the way we make it is deeply tied to our sense of self-worth and any comment can be taken in an extremely negative way. As I mentioned earlier, money is the biggest reason for couples fighting and splitting up.

However, sweeping the topic under the carpet isn't a solution either. This only leads to problems that will cause your relationship to bite the dust. Instead, it's best to prepare for it right from the beginning. Choose someone who has similar financial beliefs and spending habits that appeal to you.

No matter how much you love someone, if they tend to be loose with their money while you're thrifty, you're probably going to have major problems. Many couples find this out about one another once they're deep in a relationship and it poses a major hurdle they have to overcome.

It's best to be financially independent of your partner. This removes a lot of pressure around money the two of you will have. It also helps you spend money the way you want, without having to rationalize it to your partner. After all, it's your money and as long as you discuss this with your partner, you'll find that your relationship will be more stable.

Being independent of your partner will also avoid situations where they might potentially control you and your spending habits. While all of us have habits that can use some improvement, ceding control of your finances is something you want to avoid.

You need to have certain conversations surrounding money as early in the relationship as possible. This is simply being honest and open with your partner and it gives them the opportunity to get to know you better.

Topic #One- Financial State

Having this conversation early on is crucial to your relationship. How do you feel about being with someone who is carrying a ton of credit card debt, for example? What if they have a large amount of student loan debt? The best way to begin this conversation is to talk about yourself first.

Lay out all of your finances for them. Let them know how much you make, what your expenses are and what your debt situation is like. Keep in mind that they might not be comfortable opening up like this all at once, so you might need to have this conversation in pieces.

Whatever your approach, you need to discuss this topic in detail. This is especially relevant if you've been dating for a while and might get married in the future. Marriage has significant implications for debt and you'll learn about the legalities of this shortly. By having this conversation early you'll avoid a lot of issues.

For now, get to know each other's financial situation deeply. This isn't about judging one another. Look at it as a means of getting to know each other on a deeper level. Coming clean about your finances is an emotional act and, when done right, it will strengthen your relationship.

Topic #Two - Goals

This is another topic that you need to talk about as early as possible. Once you know each other's financial state, what are your goals? This conversation centers around what financial independence means to either one of you. You might be fine with taking a vacation to New Orleans once a year, but your partner might want to save up enough money and travel the world sometime down the world.

You might consider saving 50% of your income as a reasonable goal but your partner might think that 10% is more realistic. Your goals also tie in with whatever debt you're carrying. If your partner has student loan debt to pay off, you will need to compromise on your expenses and focus on eliminating that debt as quickly as possible.

Discuss how soon you want to get rid of debt and what your spending should be like. You will have to sacrifice on certain purchases so discuss your comfort level with foregoing these things. Again, have this conversation early!

Your money goals may not be 100% aligned with one another's and that's fine. What's more important is that you understand each other's priorities and decide on compromises that work best for the two of you.

Topic #Three - Should You Combine Finances?

This is a major decision you'll have to make and it has long-term implications. Many couples default to combining finances in a joint account but this doesn't necessarily have to be the case. I'm not suggesting that combining finances is a bad thing either. It really depends on your own situation.

If you're someone who doesn't like explaining or even approaching a situation where you need to explain your spending, combining finances might not be the best choice for you. In such situations, agreeing on budget items where expenses need to be split and contributing equally to, while maintaining separate accounts, might be the best solution.

You could have a joint account that the two of you contribute to equally every month and spend shared expenses from it. Meanwhile, you spend whatever is a personal expense from your individual accounts. A pitfall of this method is that if your partner earns far more or far less than you, you're going to have to compromise on expenses.

For example, if you can afford to rent a place for $2,000, but they can afford only $700, you're going to have to decide on how this situation will be handled. If they can afford this much because they're focused on paying off their debt, you will have to compromise. So, take the time to discuss this in detail with your partner.

Alternatively, you could have a joint account where both of you contribute equal amounts to fund a dream vacation to a destination that both of you love.

Having an open conversation about money is tough but these three topics need to be discussed for your relationship to prosper. Avoiding these conversations is only going to lead to problems down the road. Deal with them upfront and as soon as possible to avoid these issues.

While you know what topics you need to talk about, how should you bring up the subject? The way you frame your intention is very important, since using the wrong words or tone might cause your partner to think you don't trust them or that you're not confident about your own abilities to manage your money. Let's see how you can talk about money in a healthy way.

HOW TO TALK ABOUT MONEY

How you approach the subject of money is extremely important. You know what you need to talk about, so let's dive in and look at how you can avoid confrontations or misunderstandings when talking about your finances.

Compromise

There's no avoiding it. If you're going to discuss topics with your partner, you're going to have to compromise on your beliefs in certain areas. For example, your partner might want a new car but you might be wary of taking on debt, having spent years getting out of it.

This is an emotional topic and there are no right or wrong views here. Often, people get so hung up on their points of view that they forget that their partner's motivations are completely different from theirs. It is possible to practice sound financial principles and still have a different viewpoint.

So, take the time to talk about these issues with one another in detail and more importantly, communicate what your motivations are with one another. The more you talk and understand one another's motivations, the less resentment there will be when it comes to compromising.

Don't Brush it Away

Talking about money can be awkward, and many couples avoid it to the point where it turns into a fight. It's much better to talk about money regularly, and in a way where everyone gets their opinion out. You want to come to an agreement that you can both support, and that might take some time. So, talk about your money a little bit every day and immediately address the things that you're less than happy with.

Don't save it for later. This will lead you to bring it up during a heated argument and you'll end up causing more damage than you intend. It's best to avoid hurting your partner in this way and, instead, quickly bring up the things you're concerned about.

Remember that your being displeased with something doesn't justify you losing your temper or talking to your partner harshly. They might have a viewpoint that you haven't considered, so keep an open mind as much as possible.

Talk About Earning

Too many couples focus on just talking about money they need to save or budget. As I mentioned earlier, this leads to a negative mindset where you'll begin to think that money is scarce. Instead, discuss how the two of you can increase your income and how you plan on going about doing this.

Remember that your partner's threshold of financial well-being might be different from yours. They might value certain material things more (or less) than you and will want to go about attaining it in ways that might not make sense to you. As long as the two of you are open about it, and as long as you're communicating the value of these things to one another, you'll be just fine.

The point isn't to convince one another of the validity of your viewpoint. Instead, it is to focus your financial position as a team, rather than what it was individually.

Legal Implications of Getting Married

There are legal implications to marriage that you should be aware of. Most of these center around the sharing and assumption of debt. Prior to getting married, debt is the sole responsibility of the individual who assumes it. You're not responsible for your partner's debt unless you've cosigned a loan with them or if you have debt in a joint account with them.

The rules after marriage are a bit less defined. For starters, where you live dictates whether you're responsible for your spouse's debt incurred after marriage. In some states, all debt your spouse incurs after marriage is shared with you, irrespective of whether you benefited from it or whether you're even aware of it.

In some other states, common law is applied. Common law is more difficult and confusing to understand. Usually, you will not automatically assume your spouse's debt (that they incur after marriage) unless you cosign a loan document. However, if the debt is something that you benefited from, then you will be held responsible for it.

A good example of this is credit card debt that is used to pay for food or other basic needs. A trickier example is student loan debt that increased your spouse's income and thus affected your standard of living as well. Keep in mind that this beneficiary rule applies even when the debt is solely in your spouse's name.

As you can see, there are real repercussions to the way your spouse handles their finances. You could be sued by creditors, and they could go after your assets if your spouse defaults on debt. In community law states, even divorce doesn't free you from the burden of their debt. Take the time to discuss these things in advance and approach each debt individually instead of trying to go over all of these points at once.

When done well, you'll find that money can bring you and your partner closer to one another instead of being an issue.

9

AFTER GRADUATION - THE REAL WORLD

G raduation is a special day for many people. You're finally an adult and are moving into the real world. The moment is bittersweet. On one hand, you finally have your degree in your hands and it's a marker of everything you've worked for. Most of the information in this chapter pertains to college graduation, but a lot will make sense for high school graduation, too.

Depending on what you decide to do after graduation, you may be diving right into adulthood. That can be really exciting, as well as a little intimidating. Becoming, and acting and behaving like an adult, can be very freeing. The flip side is you need to finally knuckle down and start understanding how health insurance works and how car payments and credit scores work in the real world. Many students are met with a bit of a shock when they realize just how much a poor credit score hurts them and how much living expenses increase outside of school.

There are many things that you might be planning on doing once you graduate. You'll probably be earning a mature salary instead of the hourly wage that you've been earning. With more money comes greater responsibility, though. You might be tempted to buy a shiny new car, but is this really a wise decision?

You might also have plans to buy a home and get married. All of these decisions have financial implications. The bottom line for you to understand is that debt severely limits your opportunities in life. It makes everything more expensive and eliminating it should be your aim.

Remember that there is both good and bad debt. When I refer to elimination, I'm talking about removing the sources of bad debt from your life. Carrying these sources of debt could literally cost you five to six figures over the long run if you get a mortgage to buy a home ("How Debt to Income Ratio Affects Mortgages," 2020).

The first thing you might have to figure out upon graduation is how to relocate for a job or to pursue your career. If you have a job already lined up, then your company will usually pay you some money as a signing bonus. Remember that this money isn't free. Bonuses, for example, are taxed just like your regular wages - so, take that into consideration. For instance, if your new employer says that they'll include a $1,000 bonus in your first paycheck, to help with your moving expenses, you'll probably really just get 70-75% of that amount - so, $700-750, depending on how your taxes are set up.

Your withholding rate is another point to consider. Typically, employers withhold about 30% of your income automatically as taxes. Higher withholding rates mean less cash in your pocket but it also means you'll get a refund when you file your taxes. This often feels like a windfall and the lower monthly cash amounts you receive encourage you to budget wisely.

You could decrease your withholding rate and increase your monthly cash flow. However, keep in mind that you might have to pay taxes when the time comes, and this needs to be budgeted. Generally speaking, it's better to opt for a higher withholding rate so that you can rest assured that the amount withheld will take care of your tax payments.

If you haven't lined up a job as yet, you will need to budget for your job search. The IRS allows you to deduct these expenses from your taxes, so keep your receipts handy. Common expenses include travel and accommodation. You can even throw in some food expenses there. I highly recommend working with a qualified tax accountant. Their fees are usually very reasonable, and they can find ways to save you money, saving you money in the long-run.

· · ·

When searching for a job, it's a good idea to arrange a source of income for yourself even if this means you'll have less time to apply to jobs. You'll need to do this because you'll still have bills to pay. Work an hourly job or see if you can score a job with the college you graduated from.

If finding a job seems impossible, it might be a good idea to consider grad school. Not only will this boost your attractiveness as a job candidate, it will also keep you in school for two more years. Graduate degrees cost money and you'll need to apply for a scholarship to pay for this, as student loans can really crush you financially. Keep in mind, though, that not all graduate degrees are worth the added expense, unless it's specifically required for the job you want.

This is because they tend to be academically oriented and don't automatically translate to higher salaries. Avoid taking on more debt as much as possible. Many recent graduates tend to get carried away and apply for credit cards thinking their salaries will allow them to afford more luxuries.

One of the first things they often do is purchase a vehicle.

LEASE OR OWN?

One of the biggest decisions you will need to make is how you want to finance your first vehicle. Do you want to drive a fancy vehicle or are you okay with driving a less than fancy car? This boils down to whether you want to lease or own your vehicle. In automotive finance circles, this is a huge debate.

Let me make this simple for you: Never lease a car unless you can afford to flush that money down the toilet. A lease is effectively a rental payment and renting a car is one of the most expensive things you can do. Sure, you'll get to drive a fancy car for the price of owning a less desirable one but there is a way around this.

When it comes to owning a car, you need to stick to something that allows you to pay as little interest on it as possible. If you can put together $5,000 and buy a decent used car for cash, then do this. This is because a vehicle loan is a prime example of bad debt, even if you use your car to work.

The only exception here is if a fancy vehicle somehow translates into a greater level of income. Certain professions attract clients who expect some degree of flash in the professionals working in them. If you're a real estate agent and pull up in a beater, you're not going to land the sale, for instance.

For every other situation, do not assume debt when you buy a vehicle. If you have to assume debt, assume as little as possible. A car loan is bad debt because vehicle values depreciate (reduce) over time. This is also why you should never buy a new car. The minute you drive it off the dealer's lot, you'll have lost 30%!

I'm not asking you to buy the cheapest car you can find. You need to take car maintenance costs into account as well. Choose a reliable vehicle from a manufacturer with a good track record. Typically, Japanese cars hold their values well and also have a surplus of spare parts available. This means if something goes wrong, you can go to a regular mechanic to get it fixed instead of the overpriced dealer's mechanic.

If you currently are driving a car on loan, trade it in for a cheaper car and refinance the loan to reduce your monthly payment or eliminate it completely. Never pay interest on your car unless you have to.

There's also car insurance to consider. Generally speaking, men pay more than women for insurance. The fancier your car is, the more you'll pay. Newer cars are more expensive to insure than their used counterparts, too. Shop online for car insurance and choose the plan that is most affordable - this isn't necessarily the cheapest quote, but the program that will make sure your finances are safe in the case of an accident or incident. Pay attention to the terms of the contract and what's covered. Consider working with a trusted insurance broker.

You might be thinking that all of this sounds pretty restrictive. Shouldn't you enjoy your new-found freedom? Indeed, you should! This is why rentals exist. If you love cars and want to experience the thrill of a powerful engine then the best fiscal decision you can make is to rent these cars for a day or two. If you budget for entertainment, you can include this kind of expenditure for a fun day on the road.

BUYING A HOME

At some point, most people want to own their own home; it can provide a sense of security. You'll know that you'll have a roof over your head and won't have to worry about your landlord changing the terms of your lease or selling the place to another owner who wants you to move out. The best solution to all of this is to carry out what's called a house hack.

With this method, you borrow money to finance a property that contains multiple units. You live in one unit while leasing the remaining ones for rent. This way, the rent greatly subsidizes your mortgage payment and you get to own the property for a much smaller payment per month. In some cases, the rental payment might be greater than the mortgage. You can also consider purchasing a home that can be made into two units - for example, an upstairs apartment, or a garage that is converted into a rental unit.

Run the numbers carefully and consider mortgage loans from the Federal Housing Authority (FHA). FHA loans are great for first time buyers with less than perfect credit; you can also put as little as three percent down on your mortgage. This is compared to 20% down if you opt for a traditional mortgage from a bank.

The most important thing to keep in mind is that if you already have debt, you should not assume a mortgage. All of your cash, or as much of it as possible, should go towards clearing your existing debt. Only once debt is cleared should you even think of getting a mortgage, or buying very expensive assets like a home.

House hack your way forward for as long as possible until you cannot help but buy your own place to live in. This typically happens when you decide to start a family. You will need stability to raise kids and drawing a mortgage and living solely in the property in these circumstances is justified.

Qualifying for a mortgage can be tricky. They look at how much debt you have, what your income is, how much the house is worth, and your job stability - as well as your credit rating, or how well you pay your bills.

Lenders calculate your debt as a percentage of your monthly income. Anything over 40% is considered excessive. However, a percentage below this isn't a guarantee of great rates. The best thing to do is to simply eliminate or greatly reduce your debt to below 5% before applying for a mortgage.

You might be wondering: Can you apply and qualify for mortgage before you graduate? It is possible but students don't receive any preferential treatment when it comes to qualification. You'll have to provide documentary evidence of your income.

If you're working a full-time job that you qualified for after earning an associate's degree and are working towards your bachelor's, you'll stand a good chance of being approved. If you're a full-time student working a part-time job, then your income levels will be far too low for you to qualify for any significant amount.

Keep in mind that even if you qualify for a mortgage, you will need to pay the down payment and closing costs. The down payment is an amount of money your lender will require you to pay. This represents the amount that you own in your property. Typical down payment rates are 20% of the property's value.

For example, if the property you're buying is worth $100,000, you will have to pay $20,000 if you opt for a traditional mortgage. If you're applying and qualify for an FHA loan, you'll pay either $3,000 (three percent) or $10,000 (ten percent) down.

Closing costs refer to the fees you will be charged by the professionals who help you obtain and set up the mortgage. This typically amounts to three to four percent of the total value of the property. From the previous example, this means you'll have to pay $3-4,000.

This means, if you wish to buy a $100,000 home you need to have at least $7,000 in cash up to $24,000 depending on your credit score. If your dream is to own a home, start saving up right now. Make a monthly contribution into a savings account or into a CD that will allow you to hit this goal in a reasonable amount of time.

. . .

Buying a home can be a great investment but it requires proper planning. With careful budgeting and ensuring you have multiple streams of income, this can become a reality for you!

EXPECT THE UNEXPECTED

L ife is full of surprises and there's no telling what may happen tomorrow. In this book, I've given you a list of all the things you can expect. You've learned about how to save money, how you can curb overspending, your emotional triggers and you've learned how you can make money both actively and passively.

However, there's no way for me or anyone else to say what might happen tomorrow. Unforeseen events always put a strain on our finances and you need to build a buffer against these events. It's impossible to put a monetary amount on this. The best thing to do is to save an amount that makes sense to you intuitively or to save a round figure such as $3,000.

Mind you, I'm not saying this is how much you should save. Everyone has their own living standards and expenses. This fund should be in addition to saving six months' worth of living expenses. Put this into a savings account where it will earn interest.

There's no telling what sort of emergency you'll run into tomorrow. However, having this cushion will ensure that you have enough savings as cash to help tide over most emergencies.

CONCLUSION

Saving money is often thought of as being a chore. If you're making money then surely the objective should be to enjoy it! This is true. However, our expectations of what enjoyment is often is warped. We think we need to buy expensive clothes and fancy cars to truly 'enjoy' ourselves.

The fact is that our perception of what we enjoy can be managed and even changed with a few habits. The most effective way of doing this is to delay the need for instant gratification that social media creates in us. You don't have to have everything right now. Delay your gratification by a little bit and you'll notice that the smallest of things will satisfy you.

Saving money is fundamental to all of this. Even if you can save a single dollar, go ahead and do this. Congratulate yourself for saving even this amount! That single dollar can grow into a substantial amount over time. This is what compounding interest is all about. It's a snowball that rolls downhill. You end up earning interest, on your interest.

Saving money puts you on the track to get your snowball started. The best way to ensure you save money is to track it. This is what a budget does. While the budget looks pretty simple on paper, it's an extremely powerful tool that helps you become conscious of where your money is going.

You can use apps to help you prepare one or you can do it manually. Whatever your choice, make sure you have one. Do not rely on memory or some other vague tracking method. The more you track your money, the more you'll be able to figure out how to use it better.

A thing that can wreck even the most well planned budget is impulsive buying. Impulsive buying is a result of some of our deep-seated evolutionary tendencies running amok. The way to manage this habit is to simply take a few precautions and make sure the situations that trigger it are avoided.

A good example of this is to never go grocery shopping when you're hungry. Your limbic system will be primed to act in this state and will push you to buy stuff you don't need. You'll end up buying prepackaged meals that can be eaten quickly. However, these are more expensive, and they're unhealthy to boot.

Avoiding situations where you're likely to break your discipline is much better than trying to avoid temptation when it's in front of you. Structure your life so that the things that tempt you into making rash decisions are not present. Doing this requires you to figure out what your needs and wants are.

Take some time to figure this out because it cuts right to the heart of why you spend money the way you do. Reduce your spending on credit cards and work to reduce your debt in general. If you have student loans, then figure out how you can make some additional money to increase your income.

Throughout all of this remember to keep social media in its place and to not get carried away by what you see on there. It's all fake anyway and it gets you to adopt unrealistic standards. Social media creates the fear of missing out in you which in turn is related to the deep-seated herd mentality instinct within all of us.

The best way to avoid these traps is to simply refuse to indulge in the behaviors that cause them. You don't need to quit cold turkey but reduce your consumption to an hour or less every day. Throughout this time, work to improve your financial situation. Saving money is important but it works in tandem with making money.

You can save all the money you want but if you aren't making enough to cover expenses, then you're going to be left with a bunch of pennies. Conversely, you can make all the money you want but if you don't have a savings plan, you're going to be broke pretty quickly.

In this book, you've learned numerous ways by which you can make money. You now know the difference between active and passive sources of income and how they both power your wealth building efforts. While everyone wants passive sources of income, it is active sources that give you money to be able to create passive sources of wealth.

Side hustles are great active sources of money. You can use the additional cash from them to create passive businesses. Keep in mind that passive businesses might need significant time involvement upfront but this requirement eases as the businesses begin to run themselves.

A great way to save money and boost your income potential is to consider the type of degree you want to earn in college. Many professions don't require anything more than an associate's degree or even a diploma. These can have you earning a full-time salary within two years of graduating from high school.

You can then use that cash to fund your bachelor's degree which will increase your salary further. High school students can save on college tuition by enrolling in dual enrollment programs that allow you to take up to two years' worth of college classes in high school.

This will allow you to graduate sooner and you'll start earning earlier, as well. Throughout all of this, remember that dating doesn't need to break your bank account. You've learned of numerous ways to date on the cheap. In addition to this there are things to consider when you adopt a pet.

When things get serious, you'll need to be aware of all the laws surrounding debt if you get married. You'll need to use the techniques and have the three conversations surrounding money that you've learned in this book.

Lastly, it pays to start saving up for expenses you'll encounter in the real world when you're still a student. Saving up to buy a home requires substantial contributions, so start as quickly as you can. While life may throw curveballs at you, remember that with proper planning, you can reduce the negative impact of these on your life.

I'm positive this book has helped you understand not just how to save money but also how you can make more money and lead a more financially secure life. Do let me know what you think and how the information in here has helped you!

I wish you all the luck in the world and sincerely hope you reach all of your financial dreams!

GIFT FOR OUR READER

**Students' Slick Way of Saving Money Checklist
(The checklist you can't afford to go without...)**

This checklist includes:

- Top 11+ side hustle ideas for a student.
- Most recommended budgeting apps to start mapping your finances.
- Sites worth visiting for free or inexpensive textbooks, school supplies, & housing essentials.

Don't go another school year unaware of your financial situation, overspending on things you could have gotten for free, or at a ridiculous low price!

For easy access, please visit the QR code in your gift box above.

REFERENCES

Davis, J. (2020). What are the Health Benefits of Owning a Pet?. Retrieved 7 May 2020, from https://www.webmd.com/hypertension-high-blood-pressure/features/health-benefits-of-pets#1

Friedman, Z. (2020). Student Loan Debt Statistics In 2020: A Record $1.6 Trillion. Retrieved 7 May 2020, from https://www.forbes.com/sites/zackfriedman/2020/02/03/student-loan-debt-statistics/#5f950d3f281f

García, H., Miralles, F., Cleary, H., & García, H. (2016). Ikigai (2nd ed.). New York.

Heshmat, S. (2020). 10 Reasons Why People Spend Too Much. Retrieved 7 May 2020, from https://www.psychologytoday.com/us/blog/science-choice/201801/10-reasons-why-people-spend-too-much

Hess, A. (2020). College grads expect to earn $60,000 in their first job—here's how much they actually make. Retrieved 7 May 2020, from https://www.cnbc.com/2019/02/15/college-grads-expect-to-earn-60000-in-their-first-job----few-do.html

Hong, E. (2019). 5 Best Budgeting Apps. Retrieved 7 May 2020, from https://www.investopedia.com/personal-finance/personal-finance-apps/

How Debt to Income Ratio Affects Mortgages. (2020). Retrieved 7 May 2020, from https://bettermoneyhabits. bankofamerica.com/en/home-ownership/mortgage-debt-to-income-ratio

Ingraham, C. (2017). Washington Post. Retrieved 7 May 2020, from https://www.washingtonpost.com/us-policy/2019/02/19/your-friends-social-media-posts-are-making-you-spend-more-money-researchers-say/

Julson, E. (2018). 10 Best Ways to Increase Dopamine Levels Naturally. Retrieved 7 May 2020, from https://www.healthline.com/nutrition/how-to-increase-dopamine

Lake, R. (2020). If I Marry Someone With Debt Does It Become Mine? Retrieved 7 May 2020, from https://www.thebalance.com/does-marriage-make-you-responsible-for-your-partner-s-debt-4588332

Luenendonk, M. (2016). The Power Of Gratitude. Retrieved 7 May 2020, from https://www.cleverism.com/the-power-of-gratitude/

Markman, A. (2020). Comparing ourselves to others isn't as motivating as we think - Crownview Medical Group. Retrieved 7 May 2020, from https://sandiegopsychiatrist.com/comparing-ourselves-to-others-isnt-as-motivating-as-we-think/

Morse, J. (2020). 6 common causes of marital problems. Retrieved 7 May 2020, from https://bestlegalchoices.com/6-common-causes-of-marital-problems/

Murray, P. (2020). How Emotions Influence What We Buy. Retrieved 7 May 2020, from https://www.psychologytoday.com/us/blog/inside-the-consumer-mind/201302/how-emotions-influence-what-we-buy

O'Donnell, J. (2020). I Spent 15 Years Studying Why People Hate Their Jobs. This Is the Top Reason. Retrieved 7 May 2020, from https://www.inc.com/jt-odonnell/how-this-1-question-can-make-you-choose-wrong-career.html

Pet Industry Market Size & Ownership Statistics. (2020). Retrieved 7 May 2020, from https://www.americanpetproducts.org/press_industrytrends.asp

Royal, J., & O'Shea, A. (2020). What Is the Average Stock Market Return? - NerdWallet. Retrieved 7 May 2020, from https://www.nerdwallet.com/blog/investing/average-stock-market-return/

Schroeder, A. (2009). The snowball. New York: Bantam.

Social Media Addiction. (2020). Retrieved 7 May 2020, from https://www.addictioncenter.com/drugs/social-media-addiction/

Tsay, J. (2020). Is It Legal to Photocopy Textbooks?. Retrieved 7 May 2020, from https://blogs.findlaw.com/law_and_life/2014/08/is-it-legal-to-photocopy-textbooks.html

Wang, J. (2020). 7 income streams of millionaires: an open discussion of passive income. Retrieved 7 May 2020, from https://wallethacks.com/7-income-sources-streams-of-millionaires/